Slavery &

UNDERGROUND

RAILROAD

in South Central

PENNSYLVANIA

COOPER H. WINGERT

THE
History
PRESS

Published by The History Press
Charleston, SC
www.historypress.net

Copyright © 2016 by Cooper H. Wingert
All rights reserved

First published 2016

Manufactured in the United States

ISBN 978.1.46711.973.3

Library of Congress Control Number: 2015959409

CONTENTS

TO THE READER

The contents of this book hearken back to an age when freedom was not an assumption, but a privilege. When it came to the dichotomy of slavery and abolitionism, the events that unfolded in South Central Pennsylvania were a unique reflection of national progress. From the beginning, I believed that this project offered a chance to tell a national story through local history. I confined my area of focus to the four present-day counties of Cumberland, Franklin, Adams and York. I did so because the four counties compose a geographically unique area—bounded on the west by the Appalachian Mountains and the east by the Susquehanna River. These features would prove crucial both in the longevity of slavery in the region and its later distinction as a hot spot on the Underground Railroad. This is not to discount the valuable and interconnected roles played by Harrisburg, Columbia, Lancaster and other towns east of the river, which have been explored more thoroughly than the counties to the west in existing literature.

Many people have kindly and generously assisted me during the course of this project. They include Craig and Sharon Caba, Carl Dickson, John Heiser, Walter Meshaka, the staffs of the many archives and repositories I have visited and my parents. Without their collective contributions, this book would not have been possible. That said, there remains much left untold about the story of slavery and abolitionism in South Central Pennsylvania, and I hope this volume spurs even more interest and discoveries.

—Cooper H. Wingert
October 31, 2015

Chapter One

LIVES ON THE FRONTIER

The Susquehanna River flows south from upstate New York and western Pennsylvania, snaking through the ridges of the Appalachian Mountains and leaving in its path a series of abrupt mountain passes. Each of these towering ridges is a crescendo and a climax in its own, rising powerfully above all until, near river's edge, cutting steeply back to earth, marking the path of its descent with steep, rocky cliffs. By the year 1700, a mixed lot of wealthy Quakers and middling journeymen had come to stake their claim in William Penn's "Holy Experiment" called Pennsylvania. The western banks of the Susquehanna—now considered South Central Pennsylvania—were then the wild west of the known world.

His ambitions were plentiful, but Englishman John Harris knew there could be no molding of this rugged terrain when he first arrived along the banks of the Susquehanna in the early eighteenth century.[1] He had spent the last several years working in the streets of Philadelphia, doing all he could to assemble the resources for just such a journey. He would cast the fate of his entire livelihood on the banks of this river. Beyond lay scattered tribes of Native Americans, craggy mountains and great towering forests. Yet it seemed no dangers could deter his impulse to expand west.

This land, then so untamed, soon became known as the Cumberland Valley—the northerly extension of the Shenandoah Valley of Virginia. Its northern and westerly borders are marked by the towering Blue Ridge Mountain—the easternmost ridge of the Appalachian mountain range. True to its name, Blue Mountain remains a formidable wall of blue, stretching in a vastness along the northern and western edges of the wide valley. For miles, its trees blend with one another in a medley to create a bluish hue. To the east, the Susquehanna River marks another boundary. Small settlements, gristmills and other structures began to sprout along the riverbank in the years following Harris's establishment at what later became Harrisburg. Middletown (to the southeast of Harrisburg) and Carlisle (some fifteen miles west of the Susquehanna) sprang up soon after the first settlers made their trek to the region. As the safety of numbers steadily grew in the colonists' favor, great throngs would now venture farther west, into the valley.

Toward the beginning of all this, John Harris had begun a lively commerce with the local natives. His trading post, established along the eastern banks of the Susquehanna, near its confluence with Paxtang Creek, was a humble, one-story log residence, where he lived with his recent bride and growing family. Revered among the natives as a brewer of alcohol, his trading post became a routine stop for men of both races. Congregating within, natives and the occasional white traveler would barter with Harris, or one another, for a variety of goods. Once a deal was agreed upon, Harris, or perhaps someone else, would go to retrieve the items from nearby sheds overflowing with a variety of skins and furs—among other things—that he had bartered from natives.

Life in this frontier land required a wide range of necessities, and Harris's trading post was prepared to meet all of them, functioning a lot like a general store. The Englishman was known to have muskets, along with several barrels of gunpowder and dozens of pounds of bar lead, ready to be melted for musket balls, flints, oxen shirts, garland shirts, hatchets, "looking glasses" (an equivalent of binoculars), knives, razors, equipment for horses and much more.[2]

In the final years of Harris's life, a swashbuckling, fearless young Irishman dared to go even further. George Croghan wasted no time in involving himself in the Indian trade upon his arrival in the colony in 1741. Whereas Harris had set up shop on the Susquehanna's eastern banks some twenty years prior, Croghan boldly marched himself across the river to what was then Pennsborough township in Lancaster County. There was good money to be made in the profitable Indian trade, especially in Pennsylvania, as evidenced by John Harris. Manufacturers as near as Lancaster and Philadelphia, and others as distant as London and Bristol, were in constant demand for the furs and skins obtained from the North American wilderness. A wide variety of goods would be shuffled down the chain of credit until finally in the hands of the traders themselves, who would barter such things as gunpowder, blankets, stockings and countless other European products for the prizes hunted by the natives.

A hard drinker with a flamboyance unbecoming of a partly illiterate, poor Irish rogue, Croghan used all his tact to earn the trust of the natives, who now inhabited the vast, uncharted region to the west of the Appalachian Mountains. As testaments to his good intentions, he learned the Delaware and Iroquois languages, treated native chiefs with the respect of dignitaries and made key allies among the natives through fair trading and reputable dealings. Croghan's success in the Indian trade—due in no small part to his congeniality—took off rapidly. He had come to the Americas in 1741 with next to nothing, and by October 1745 he was able to purchase a 354-acre tract of land running along the Conodoguinet Creek in Pennsborough township, where he built a log house near the banks of the creek. For those travelers who continued westward past Harris's Ferry, their next stop would be at Croghan's plantation. He raised crops, striving to be as self-sufficient as possible, and grazed his horses and cattle in the fertile fields bordering the creek. On a smaller tract of land, he operated a tannery, where he processed many of the furs and skins acquired through his trading activities. Like Harris, he also operated a general store, where travelers could purchase from a large variety of day-to-day necessities and Native American goods.

Croghan was rarely home. He might be in Shippensburg, another center of his trading operations, or out on one of his many daring expeditions into the vast region beyond the mountains. For his trading activities, he usually took a route that emanated directly from his plantation house to the nearby mountain gap, which then bore his name. Croghan's Gap (later Sterrett's Gap) led Croghan and those accompanying him over the Blue Ridge Mountains and into Sherman's Valley, where he followed the Juniata and Conemaugh Rivers farther west.[3] Life in this unrelenting stretch of land between the Susquehanna and the Blue Ridge embraced all the hardships fathomable to the human psyche, yet it was a life men like Croghan and Harris choose willingly. No danger, it seems, could outweigh the adventure, the thrill—or the profit.

These lifestyles in mind, few would link the frontier bravado of Harris and Croghan with the popular image of American slavery. Its legacy, as commonly taught, imprints on our minds an image of hundreds of African slaves, sweating profusely, hunched over as they pick cotton in some vast, flat plantation. That concept of slavery is further silhouetted with the knowledge that this mass slave labor took place in the sweltering clime of the American South, where slavery formed the brunt of the economic wealth and defined social statuses in the years leading up to the Civil War. True as this may be, this over-simplified idea of slavery in North America leaves much untold. Take, for instance, that both Harris and Croghan owned and employed slaves in South Central Pennsylvania. Couple that with the reality that eighteenth-century Pennsylvanians imported thousands of slaves during a period spanning many decades. Slavery and its dehumanizing features existed in Pennsylvania, and all thirteen of the original colonies. "The peculiar institution" was, from the very start, an American problem—not just a Southern problem.

Hercules was the slave of John Harris. He had no last name—not that we know of, at least. This was not uncommon among African-descent slaves throughout the thirteen colonies. If they ever were lucky enough to live as freemen, most would simply assume their master's last name, if they took any at all. Hercules, it appears, was no different.

John Harris apparently purchased Hercules shortly after he first settled on the banks of the Susquehanna. Hercules is a towering figure in the annals of the Harris settlement, largely thanks to the legend of the mulberry tree. The highly debated "burning" of John Harris occurred when the English trader refused to give rum to a group of traveling Native Americans. The *"whoop of revenge* echoed through the wilderness," and Harris was yanked out and tied to a nearby mulberry tree, where they prepared to burn him alive. At the critical juncture, Hercules, who was on the west shore at the time, quickly alerted friendly natives, who then rushed across the river just in time to save his master.[4]

We will probably never know if John Harris was ever tied to a mulberry tree and threatened to be burned. Nor may we ever be certain that Hercules—one of the first slaves brought to the region—ushered friendly natives across the river just in the nick of time to save the very man who held him in bondage. Yet for the dramatic rescue he may or may not have executed, Hercules received acclaim and renown among locals for the remaining decades of his life. Throughout the mid-eighteenth century, the attention of countless travelers through Harris's Ferry was directed to the old, black man fishing in the river. They were told that he was Hercules and that he had saved the life of his master from the natives. Perhaps they were alluding to the local folklore of the mulberry tree—or perhaps to another alleged incident, in which Hercules was said to have saved Harris's life during a river flat accident. Either way, the recurring mythology and Harris's own actions prove, beyond reasonable doubt, there was an affection between John Harris and his slave. He would later will that "my negro man Hercules be sett [*sic*] free & be allowed to live on a part of the tract…left to my son William."

Harris's manumission of Hercules had not changed his views on slavery as an institution. In that same document, he divided among his children "the negro Boy called Tom," "the negro girl called Cherida" and even "the child whereof the negro woman is now pregnant."[5] Hercules, too, though free and on amicable terms with the Harris family, continued to labor in the fields and crossings surrounding Harris's Ferry for years after achieving his legal freedom. Account books for John Harris Jr. show Hercules continuing to do work—and receiving pay for it—from the 1750s until as late as the 1770s.[6]

George Croghan, the gruff Indian trader, also employed slaves in his operations on the very frontier of South Central Pennsylvania. At his plantation along the Conodoguinet, he had both indentured servants and African-descent slaves who took care of the pack animals, supervised the crops he grew and likely assisted in his tannery. They also routinely accompanied him westward over the mountains on his trading expeditions.[7] Neither Croghan nor Harris would be the last slaveholder to venture west of the Susquehanna—they were merely among the first to drag bondsmen into a new territory that would soon be transformed.

Chapter Two

THE QUAKER COLONY

Pennsylvania's ties to slavery go back before there ever was a Pennsylvania. Admiral William Penn, the father of the colony's founder, had seized Jamaica in 1655 for England. Admiral Penn's victory would only whet Britain's taste for slave labor—the island's sweltering climate made it perfect for large-scale, plantation-style agriculture. It was this glorious conquest that, in turn, furnished his son, William Penn, with the massive land charter in 1681, which became Pennsylvania.[8]

The younger Penn decided to keep his new colony open to persons of all faiths. It was a choice that would put Pennsylvania front and center in the New World as one of the most attractive colonies for emigrants who were not necessarily wealthy or among the cliques of the European elite. Those who sailed for Pennsylvania were generally middle class; neither wealthy nor impoverished, they usually excelled at a certain trade—perhaps as a farmer, a craftsmen or an artisan. These diverse ethnic backgrounds shared the same uniting belief that with hard work and dedication they could stand on their own feet. To Pennsylvania they had come to escape the thralls of medieval serfdom, where many faced a life doomed to repetitive labor, largely for the benefit of lords and nobles. In Pennsylvania, they were determined to chart a course for their own advancement. Not surprisingly, most colonists set up dispersed family farms, where they were most concerned with maintaining connections with major trading hubs rather than being in a community setting.[9]

Slavery had been sanctioned by the church for thousands of years. What made Pennsylvania unique, however, was an evolving interpretation of the scriptures—an effort spearheaded by a few factions of Quakers. Pennsylvania was still a Quaker colony, and not surprisingly, the "Holy Experiment" was guided immensely by Quaker philosophies. What had long justified human bondage was the idea of original sin, which held that sin, a slavery of the soul, justified the physical act of enslaving a human being. Quaker philosophy challenged this very concept. Not only were Friends enamored with Enlightenment ideas, but as pacifists, many were offended by the brutality involved in enslaving humans and forcibly holding them in bondage. This train of thought, however, at first belonged to only a few fringe elements within the Quaker community. Indeed, wealthy Friends were among the largest slaveholders in colonial Pennsylvania. However, it was the gradual growth of this new belief that sowed the seeds for upheaval to come.[10]

In 1684, a slave ship brought 150 Africans to the newly settled city of Philadelphia, who were quickly sold among its 2,000 residents.[11] Slavery was nothing new to the Friends running the affairs of the new colony; for decades, Quaker missionaries had been making frequent trips to Barbados, where they converted scores of slaveholding plantation owners. Quaker merchants in Philadelphia relied on many of those same West Indies farmers for the slave-produced goods they would sell. These merchants also made a habit of applying credit leftover from sales of any number of goods—barrels of flour, herring or grain—to purchase cheaper slaves who were no longer in demand by the Caribbean planters. These men and women, who were labeled with terms such as "refuse" or "waste," had apparently not lived up to the lofty demands of their masters in the unrelenting West Indies plantation economy. For the most part, these "refuse" slaves were the only Africans actively purchased by Pennsylvanians during the first quarter of the eighteenth century. The colony's natural climate lacked the extreme temperatures that were needed to cultivate a staple crop like tobacco, cotton, indigo or sugar cane. Devoid of the economic incentive, Pennsylvanians simply could not compete with Southern buyers for what were considered the strongest, fittest and ablest slaves.

Even well-to-do Pennsylvania farmers were reluctant to take the risk of purchasing a slave. When confronted with the choice of a white indentured servant, freshly arrived from Europe, or a "refuse" slave, Pennsylvanians generally chose the former. They required labor for small farms, not industrial-like plantations, which led them to prefer a temporary white laborer from Europe over a slave for life. Additionally, the purchase of a slave was a big economic risk. During the 1720s, the average price for a male slave was forty-five pounds, and the risk of that man running away was often too great a concern for many Pennsylvanians. For these reasons, from 1690 to 1720, most Pennsylvanians would see only a small dribbling of slaves. These Africans arrived at Philadelphia in sporadic spurts—sometimes individually, on account of a specific request carried out by a merchant with his contact in the West Indies, or other times in small groups of several bondsmen. With a steady supply of cheap, although temporary, white labor, there was no urgent need to pay out large sums up front for a more permanent source.[12]

The path being charted by Quaker theologians and the gradual growth of slavery in the colony were bound to collide soon enough. Just a few years before, founding Quaker George Fox had gone to the plantation metropolis of Barbados to advise slaveholding Friends to free their slaves "after a considerable [t]erm of [y]ears, if they have served them faithfully." Not only that, Fox added that "when they go, and are made free, *let them not go away empty-handed.*" He asked plantation owners to "consider…if you were in the same [c]ondition as the [b]lacks are…who came as [s]trangers to you, and were sold to you as Slaves; now I say, if this should be the [c]ondition of you or yours, you [would] think it hard [m]easure; yea, and very great Bondage and Cruelty."

"[C]onsider seriously of this," he added, reminding his audience of the so-called golden rule, "and do…to them, as you would willingly have them or any other do unto you, were you in the like slavish [c]ondition."[13] Although, at the time, Quakers on both sides of the Atlantic still accepted slavery as an institution, Fox and other Friends were clearly flirting with ideas that rendered slavery a contradiction. It was no coincidence that Quaker-dominated Pennsylvania would be among the first places to see those ideas play out in the court of public opinion and ultimately the first place where they would come to fruition.

In 1696, after a small but impactful scuffle over the morality of the slave trade, the Philadelphia Yearly Meeting advised its members "not to Encourage the bringing in of any more Negroes, & that such that have Negroes be Careful of them." This rather feeble suggestion did not make any significant waves, and many Friends continued to actively own, purchase and import slaves. A few years later, in 1712, Friend William Southeby petitioned the Pennsylvania Assembly to abolish slavery on the heels of a violent slave insurrection in neighboring New York. The assembly shot down Southeby's proposal, deeming it "neither just nor convenient."[14] Over the coming decades, activist Friends such as Ralph Sandiford and Benjamin Lay

As early as the seventeenth century, founding Quaker George Fox urged his followers to treat their slaves with humanity and benevolence. *Library of Congress.*

applied personal influence and strange tactics in attempts to motivate their fellow Friends. Lay, the eccentric hunchback, made his feelings about slavery known to any and all slaveholders upon his arrival in Pennsylvania. He shocked wealthy Quakers who expected civility with blunt admonishments about the sins of slaveholding.

Lay was a fan of the bizarre, and besides his hermit-like, vegetarian lifestyle, his quirks were on full display at Quaker meetinghouses in eastern Pennsylvania. On one snowy night, he stood outside the entrance with his right leg bare and in the snow. Several Friends were quick to chide Lay about the dangers of exposure, to which he replied, "Ah you pretend compassion for me, but you do not feel for the poor slaves in your fields, who go all winter half clad." Another time, Lay entered a meetinghouse with a vessel filled with pokeberry juice concealed underneath two coats. He rambled off a few words about the "self-interested custom" of slaveholding, and then, grasping a sword from his side, he pierced the container of juice, splattering it upon those seated nearby.[15] Lay's antics made few friends at the time, but bluntness like his helped move forward the conversation among Quaker circles and, years later, inspired generations of future abolitionists.

Chapter Three

SLAVERY AND THE RISE OF SOUTH CENTRAL PENNSYLVANIA

The slaves of George Croghan were among the first African bondsmen to live on the western banks of the Susquehanna. In the years to follow, settlers would migrate in droves to the fertile nook that became South Central Pennsylvania, establishing family farms alongside a scattering of small towns. For some time, the region had remained a part of Lancaster County, but as more people flocked to the region, government from the opposite shore became all but impossible. In 1750, the land west of the Susquehanna and north of South Mountain was sectioned off and christened Cumberland County.

The new county ran the length of the Cumberland Valley in Pennsylvania—from the banks of the Susquehanna opposite Harris's Ferry, curving with the mountains down to the Maryland border. York County, established a year prior, claimed a smaller foothold on the southern side of South Mountain, also bordering Maryland. The two counties thus created would be largely unrecognizable today. Cumberland County then included within its bounds present-day Cumberland, Perry and Franklin Counties, as well as the greater part of the uncharted land to the west. York encompassed a smaller territory, within the modern limits of York and Adams Counties.

Settlers in the Cumberland Valley found the prospect of shipping their goods to market in Philadelphia vexing, not only because it lay some one hundred or more miles to the east, but also considering the difficulties involved in ferrying goods across the mile-wide Susquehanna. The river would not be bridged until half a century later. This environmental barrier shifted the attention of most farmers to the more convenient market of Baltimore. It follows, rather logically, that the economic interests of the men and women located west of the river were tied more closely than any other part of Pennsylvania to the neighboring, slaveholding meccas of Maryland; Washington, D.C.; and Virginia. Carriage making quickly became the prime business in Gettysburg, and a great number of distinctive "Gettysburg carriages" produced there were sold into neighboring Maryland and Virginia.

Economic ties coincide with frequent travel, and with that comes exposure. Most men and women in South Central Pennsylvania, if they lived anytime in the century spanning 1760–1860, would have borne some form of familiarity with slavery—be it from owning slaves themselves or having witnessed it. The earliest residents would have grown up observing and living among the one-thousand-plus slaves who populated the region. Those who came later, born after the 1830s, may not have seen slavery itself on Pennsylvania soil, but they would have still seen its traces. They would have read about fugitive slaves in the newspapers, almost on a weekly basis; they probably knew or maybe even employed free blacks. Perhaps they had gone south, into Maryland or northern Virginia, on a business-related trip, or maybe they had seen a slave brought north temporarily with his southern master. Regardless, multiple generations of South Central Pennsylvanians would bear witness to slavery, in one form or another. The crucial factor at play was how such contact affected those individuals living in the valley. It would lead to heated debates, covert activity and even violence. For much of the eighteenth and nineteenth centuries, South Central Pennsylvania remained something of a borderland—a violent medley between slavery and freedom.

During the colonial years, wealthy farmers eager to display their fortunes were generally the ones to purchase slaves, sometimes for personal or household use, or other times for work on their plantation—a large, several-hundred-acre farm by Pennsylvania standards. Pennsylvanians overwhelmingly preferred to buy young slaves, especially boys and girls in their early teens. Those who sought slave labor usually requested a "young Negroe man" or "boy" and oftentimes when searching for household servants a "young Negroe girl." A 1737 ship docking in Philadelphia, straight from South Carolina, advertised "a parcel of likely Young Negro Boys and Girls." This clear preference toward younger slaves was the result of fears that older bondsmen—even those in their twenties—were either too old to learn a trade or too "dishonest" and "corrupted" to be faithful servants.

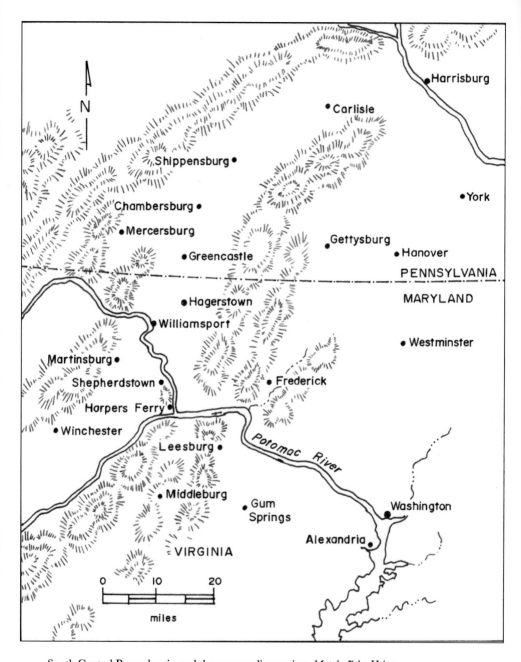

South Central Pennsylvania and the surrounding region. *Map by John Heiser.*

Racist views had dissipated among Pennsylvanians both rich and poor, and those of African descent were often spoken of in contemporary accounts as drunken, disorderly, incompetent and altogether unintelligent. When seeking to purchase a bondsmen, potential buyers repeatedly specified that he or she be honest, diligent and, most of all, sober.[16] Those seeking to sell slaves would take care to exemplify these qualities, such as this 1749 notice:

> TO BE SOLD
> *A Likely Negroe man, about 18 years of*
> *age, fit for town or country business, and has had*
> *the small pox. Enquire at the Post-Box.*[17]

Settlers in South Central Pennsylvania would see their lifestyles radically change in the mid-1750s with the onset of the French and Indian War. For this new war on the American frontier, British forces lured hundreds of indentured servants into the ranks. Many of these white laborers simply left their masters, often unannounced. This new reality forced men throughout the colony to turn to slave labor, whether they wanted to or not and in spite of the prejudices held by many. Representatives in the general assembly made clear the widespread reluctance among Pennsylvanians, lamenting that when servants were recruited "in the Midst of Harvest or of Seed-time…the People [will be] driven to the Necessity of providing themselves with Negro slaves, as the Property in them and their Service seems at present more secure." Beginning in the late 1750s and continuing throughout the next decade, Philadelphia merchants sent ships directly to the African coastline seeking new bondsmen. No longer were Pennsylvanians content with the "refuse" slaves of the West Indies. The Quaker colony was now importing slaves directly on its own vessels.[18]

The surge in imported slaves would also trigger renewed efforts from a new generation of abolitionists. To Friend John Churchman, the brutalities of warfare so near the home front were shocking. As he wandered through the streets of Philadelphia in deep contemplation, Churchman watched in horror as wagons arrived carrying bodies of slain men. How could this be, he asked? Pennsylvania had long been "a land of peace, and as yet not much concerned in war," he reasoned, "but as it were in a moment mine eyes were turned to the case of the poor enslaved Negroes: And however light a matter they who have been concerned with them may look upon the purchasing, selling, or keeping of those oppressed people in slavery, it then appeared plain to me, that such were partakers in iniquity, encouragers of war and the shedding of innocent blood, which is often the case, where those unhappy people are or have been captivated and brought away for slaves." It was through the "sins of the inhabitants…that the Lord has suffered this calamity and scourge to come upon them."[19]

The pieces of the puzzle were indeed coming together throughout much of the Quaker community to spearhead a push for abolitionism. As war engulfed Pennsylvania, many Quakers were forced out of government because of their pacifist beliefs, allowing them to focus anew on the affairs of their faith. In the meantime, a number of Friends underwent moral epiphanies that changed their views, although many did not—as evidenced by the tenacity with which some Quakers held on to their slaves, despite overtures from their church. John Woolman had his moral epiphany sometime earlier, in 1743, when his employer asked him to draw up a bill of sale for a slave woman. "The thing was [s]udden," recalled Woolman, "and though the thoughts of writing an Instrument of Slavery for one of my fellow creatures felt uneasie, yet I remembered I was hired by the year…so through weakness I gave way, and wrote it, but at the [e]xecuting it I was so [a]fflicted in my mind, that I said…that I believed Slavekeeping to be a practice inconsistent with the Christian Religion."[20] Many of the older, slave-owning Quakers had been gradually replaced by a new generation of Friends. Positions such as Overseers of the Press—an influential group that decided which tracts written by Friends could be published—were now in the hands of abolitionists, not slaveholders. Partial success finally came to fruition in the 1758 Philadelphia Yearly Meeting, when the Society of Friends threatened to discipline any Friend who bought, imported or sold slaves—notwithstanding, slaveholding itself was still allowed.[21]

Yet just as antislavery Quakers finally prevailed in Philadelphia, many miles to the west, slavery was beginning anew, in the fertile Cumberland Valley. Come 1750, newly minted Cumberland County was home to no more than a few thousand men and women. Lying to the south, York County contained only a few more.[22] From the beginning, settlers to this region were desperately hungry for labor. The first sources of labor came from within the family unit itself, where fathers and mothers tasked their sons with work varying from clearing land to tilling or plowing fields or building homes, outbuildings or barns. Daughters would be entrusted with a variety of domestic tasks from gardening to weaving to cooking. However, the tasks of building homes and barns, clearing and tilling land and defending oneself from hostile natives or even lawlessness were tall asks for any family to answer alone. Most who could afford the upfront cost quickly began purchasing slaves to complement their labor force. Some contracted indentured servants—and then others sought both. George Croghan had engaged an assortment of slaves and indentured servants for labor as early as the 1740s.

Slave ownership was by and large limited to the upper stratums of this emerging rural society. Most early slave owners in Cumberland and York Counties likely purchased their slaves nearer Philadelphia. A wealthy man would typically own only one or two slaves, and usually their tasks would fall according to gender. Female slaves usually were given household duties, such as cooking, cleaning and maintenance. Males were tapped for a wide variety of tasks, and they usually reflected their master's occupation. Many tavern keepers employed male slaves, as did farmers and even carpenters. The small number of slaves and their close proximity meant they very often lived and slept in the very same house as their white counterparts and at times developed close relationships. Most men who were not considered wealthy for their time sought the labor of indentured servants and only if their children could not supply the requisite labor.

Robert Dunning was typical of the early South Central Pennsylvania slaveholder. Unlike the popular image of American slavery, Dunning did not relentlessly work his slaves for large profits but rather entrusted them with everyday tasks necessary for the survival of both themselves and his family. Life in the partly settled Cumberland Valley held no guarantees, and difficulties could arise anywhere from hostile natives to insufficient food. By 1750, Dunning was ill, and fearing an imminent death, he drafted his will—the first to be filed in Cumberland County. "To my wife Mary Dunning, for my daughters—I leave my negro Whiteball, and the negro woman Phillis—to help raise bread for the maintenance of our children."[23]

John Williamson was not far off from Dunning. A clothier from Lurgan township, Williamson likely tasked his male slave Cesar with everything from mundane household duties to helping produce various apparel items for sale or barter. In his will, he bequeathed to his wife "my Negro slave Cesar."[24] Much of the same could be said of John Blair, a Fannett township resident who willed that upon his death, much of his land "together with my Negro Man and Woman and all the moveable Estate be sold at the discretion of my Executors." He also bequeathed to his son-in-law "a young Negro Boy called Bob," whom he no doubt intended to be a life servant for his son-in-law, considering the age of the "young Negro Boy."[25]

Yet the story is different when it comes to Philip Davis of Peters township, who made his will around the same time but had settled farther south down the valley than Dunning, Williamson or Blair. Davis resided on a massive farm he referred to as "my plantation," which included his self-described "mansion house." He had two sons and four daughters, and in his will he managed to leave each and every one of his children with a slave, including one for his wife, Sarah. Philip Davis, therefore, owned no fewer than seven slaves (three males and four females) in 1753 at his Cumberland County plantation. Unique among the early slaveholders, Davis willed his "Negro Wench named Mary" to wife Sarah, with further instructions that upon Sarah's death Mary was either to be willed to a grandchild, "or else to set her altogether free." Alongside John Harris, Philip Davis was tacitly acknowledging the contradictions of bondage as he made out his will, leaving one of his slaves with a potential pathway to freedom, while six more—males Jack, George and Will and females Dinah, Kitt and Jean—were, as far as Philip Davis was concerned, destined for lives of servitude among his six children.[26]

Not far from Davis was the plantation of Henry P. Pawling, in neighboring Antrim township. Although Pawling himself died in the early 1760s, an inventory of his estate conducted in 1763 provides crucial insight into the lives of the men and women who labored for him during the 1760s and earlier. Pawling's 657-acre plantation included half a dozen horses, more than two dozen cattle and eight slaves. Also recorded in the inventory is "a bed for the Negroes" valued at a mere fifteen shillings—this compared to beds used by the Pawling family that were valued at as much as six pounds and ten shillings. Unlike other inventories of beds taken in the household, there is no bed stand included with this description—leading to the likelihood that it was at best a crude bed laying on the floor. Although the inventory does not give a positive location for this bed, it is listed among hogsheads, tin quarts, knives and forks, pots and skillets and bread baskets, which suggests that Pawling's slaves slept in the kitchen.[27]

At the other end of Cumberland County, Robert Callender—a fur trader and cohort of George Croghan—resided in East Pennsborough in 1766 with five slaves and four indentured servants. Deeply in debt for much of his later life, Callender nonetheless clung tenaciously to the labor that maintained his lifestyle. When he was not out bartering with Native Americans or captaining a company of militia, Callender sought respite at his sizable plantation located a few miles inland from the river. There his slaves and indentured servants labored each day in the upkeep of nearly a dozen horses, even more cattle and his gristmill. He had two hundred acres cleared but five times that patented. On top of running the existing farm, he probably put his slaves to work clearing this additional acreage.

The early 1770s saw Callendar relocate a few miles farther west, northeast of Carlisle in Middleton township.[28] In the intervening time, the gentleman planter moved increasingly away from indentured servants to depending almost solely on slave labor. By the time of his 1776 death, Callendar's estate included no fewer than eight slaves. Callendar's apparent favorite was William, or Bill, who was himself a mulatto—a commonly used term indicating that a slave was the product of one white parent and one black parent. Other slaves included a man named Casteel; a woman named Gin and her young son Ben; three more boys named York, Bill and Jerry; and, finally, a girl, Hanna. In his will, Callendar manumitted Bill, who "is to be free immediately after my decease." The rest of his slaves remained in bondage for years to come under the ownership of his widow, Frances, as

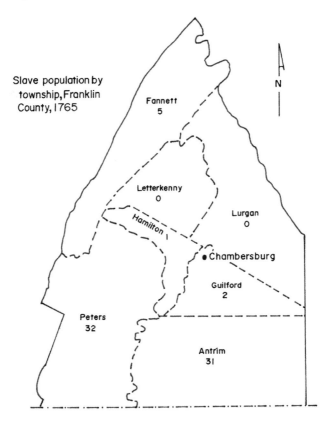

Slave owners John Williamson, John Blair and Philip Davis resided in the lower half of Cumberland County, within what later became Franklin County (established 1784). In 1765, slave populations were concentrated at the southern end of the valley, near the Maryland border, in Peters and Antrim townships. These figures signify the number of bondsmen taxed, which usually fell short of the actual total. *Map by John Heiser.*

did "a black woman named Nell," who he had previously given "as a gift to my sister for her separate use."[29]

Come 1765, tax records reveal around 145 slaves in Cumberland County, compared to some 94 indentured servants. However, tax collectors made a habit of not taxing every slave, usually neglecting to tally those who were either very young or very old. All considered, there were probably close to 200 slaves, if not more, living in Cumberland County as of 1765.[30] From the very beginning, these men and women held in bondage caught glimpses of runaway slaves from farther south passing through the area—many trying to make for the large free black community in Philadelphia.

When his slave Scipio ran away in early 1749, Maryland slave owner Thomas Prather waited—like many slave owners did—for cooler heads to prevail and hoped Scipio would return on his own. Several months later, however, he learned that Scipio had made his way north, up the Susquehanna to Harris's Ferry. "It is said that the said Negroe was, about two months ago; at Mr. Harris's, on the Susquehannah, and wanted to come to Philadelphia to be safe; that he had a pass with him, and pretended to be a free-man." So wrote Prather that July, when he finally gave in and published an advertisement for Scipio's return in the Philadelphia-printed *Pennsylvania Gazette*. He was of "short stature, plays on the Banjo, and can sing." Perhaps even more significant were the friends Prather had. "Whoever takes up said slave, and brings him to Mr. George Croghan, or Mr. George Gibson, in Lancaster, or to Marcus Kuhl, in Philadelphia; shall have Three Pounds reward, and reasonable charges, paid by George Croghan, George Gibson, Marcus Kuhl."[31] This statement from the Marylander demonstrates that, as early as the 1740s, Southern slave owners had formed relationships with prominent Pennsylvanians, some of whom were slaveholders themselves.

The first runaway ads from South Central Pennsylvania slaveholders would not begin to appear in the far-off *Pennsylvania Gazette* until the early 1760s. Yet it remains all but certain that the region's oppressed African-descent populace had been testing the boundaries of freedom from the very beginning. A fall 1763 notice is among the earliest surviving ads, in which Thomas Butler of Carlisle sought a runaway "Negroe Man, of middle Size, and middle Age" named Abel, a tradesmith. "Had on when he went away, an Elkskin Jacket, Buckskin Breeches, pieced on the Knee[s], Shoes and Stockings." Butler offered a forty shilling reward.[32] Abel was returned, and in the intervening years, Butler moved farther to the west, to West Pennsborough township. Resolute in his thirst for liberty, Abel would embark on another run for freedom in July 1770.[33]

Iron collars had long been employed by slave owners, serving as both a working irritation device and a clear delineation of slave status. *J. Howard Wert Gettysburg Collection.*

In 1764, Carlisle slaveholder John Gemmil advertised a runaway "Negroe Lad, named Abraham, about 19 Years of Age, 5 feet high, this Country born." Abraham was a skilled laborer and, according to his master, "can do a little in Silver Work, [and] is active in any Kind of Farming Business." Abraham's appearance certainly would have drawn attention as he made his way through the countryside, toward either Philadelphia or Baltimore. He was wearing "an Iron Collar, Blanket Coat, Buckskin Breeches, Stockings, and Shoes with Whitemetal Buckles."[34]

Abraham, like a handful of other documented slaves in colonial Cumberland County, bore African tribal markings on his ears. Yet like many others who had these markings, Abraham was reported by his master to have been "this Country born"—a testament that in the Pennsylvania countryside, the enslaved African community carried on traditions from another continent for at least one generation, if not more, removed from their homeland. When advertising for the return of Abel, Thomas Butler expressed his belief that "a bit hath been taken out of his ear."[35] These tribal markings appear to have been more prevalent among South Central Pennsylvania's African-descent population during the early colonial years. This makes sense, considering these traditions were likely passed down by those who had lived in Africa at some point in their lives. As time and the generations wore on, however, these particular traditions by and large appear to have disappeared. One of the latest recorded mentions of tribal markings comes from a forty-year-old slave from neighboring Dauphin County in 1794, who was reported to be "scarred on each cheek with the mark of his country."[36]

Skin color was given an important emphasis in the emerging rural society of South Central Pennsylvania. Slaves were consistently classified as either "Negro" or "Mulatto." Although both were treated as inferior races, there were clear and repeated efforts made to delineate between the two. A 1769 advertisement from York County warned readers that a fugitive "is very yellow, and has passed for a Mulattoe."[37] At Peach Bottom Ferry, in southern York County, Hugh Whiteford sought the return of "a *Mulattoe* slave, named

Jack, about 22 years of age, well set, about 5 feet 5 inches high, and very white of the sort."[38]

Multiple runaway ads from York County spoke of "a Negroe *Man*, who calls himself *Moses Grimes*, about 5 feet 4 or 5 inches high, about 29 years of age." At first mention, Grimes was committed to the York jail in 1764, when, in his mid-twenties, he was traveling alone with a horse, claiming to be a freeman. Five years later, Grimes resurfaces as a slave to Philip Graybill in downtown York. This begs the possibility that Grimes was a freeman after all, or perhaps a runaway from a distant region, and when no master came to claim him, Grimes was sold at auction by the jailer to pay for his prison charges. Nevertheless, in March 1769, Grimes made a run for freedom from his new master.

Evidently, he was recaptured soon afterward and sold (no doubt for being a headache to Graybill) to Thomas Minshall, residing along the Susquehanna at Wright's Ferry. Just three months later, Grimes fled from his new owner in July 1769. Whereas previous runaway ads taken out on Grimes featured nothing out of the ordinary, Minshall unleashed a verbal tirade against the freedom-seeking man. Moses Grimes "is very talkative, and given to lying," warned Minshall. He "used to be an hostler, and to wait in a tavern...it is likely that he will pass for a free man, and get somebody to forge a pass for him."

Once again, Grimes was recaptured, but Minshall was forced to advertise for him again in May 1770. By then, six years after he was first recorded in the annals of history, Moses Grimes was described as "about 30 years of age, about 5 feet 5 inches high, his head is a little bald, very talkative, a great liar, this country born, and will pass for a free Negroe." This time, Grimes had company during his flight, in the form of a mason's apprentice.

The name Moses Grimes appears one last time in the pages of the *Pennsylvania Gazette*, two years later in November 1772. The description of this Moses Grimes—who by 1772 had become a slave to Philadelphian John Hales—is nearly identical. This Moses Grimes was "about 32 years of age, about 5 feet 6 inches high, of a yellowish complexion, the fore part of his head shaved, and is rather bald, he sometimes wears a wig." In all likelihood, this was the same Moses Grimes who had run away from multiple masters over the past decade in York County—and it only fit more with his previous behavior for him to make a run for freedom once again. After no doubt earning the ire of Thomas Minshall for running away twice, he was apparently sold to Hales in Philadelphia.

Hales gives several more details about Grimes, noting that he "is very religious, preaches to his colour, walks before burials, and marries; he is very artful, pretends to be free, and will no doubt get a forged pass; he is very fond of liquor, and if spoke familiarly to pretends to simplicity and laughs." Perhaps most significant, however, was where Hales believed Moses Grimes was headed: "It is supposed he is gone to…Carlisle in this province," he added in his advertisement. The fact that Grimes would be expected to make a westward trek into the backcountry indicates he may have had connections there. If anything, his unrelenting efforts to gain his freedom reveal Moses Grimes as a man who refused to bow down, even to the most powerful and daunting suppression thrown at him. Grimes made clear that although oppressed, South Central Pennsylvania's African-descent community would not submit to slavery.

Chapter Four

REVOLUTIONARY TIMES

Doctor Jonathan Calhoon had spent much of his early career in Shippensburg, but it was his marriage to Ruhamah—the daughter of Colonel Benjamin Chambers—that brought him to Chambersburg. In the midst of the Revolution, John and Ruhamah settled in a white weatherboard house situated at the northeast corner of Main and King Streets. Their home was laden with supplies for his practice, housing a wide selection of medical equipment from various salts to a large grouping of plant-based extracts known as gums, which were chewed by Doctor Calhoon's patients to counter any number of medical maladies. Countless vials, medical bottles and probes lay about, too; he also owned a syringe, a marble mortar and pestle and, finally, three saws and a blade.

The spaces where John and Ruhamah lived were filled with possessions befitting a prominent valley physician. They had two dining tables and an assortment of Windsor, leather-bottom and blue-wash chairs to accompany it. A child's high chair was added to the mix as John and Ruhamah's family continued to grow. Ruhamah had a tea table, where she entertained guests, while several times a day John would sit down at his desk to read and reply to correspondence and tabulate his finances. In his late thirties, Doctor Calhoon could count on a heavy stack of correspondence to sift through each day, dealing with everything from his medical practice to the paper mill he was constructing in town, the first of its kind west of the Susquehanna.

There were multiple beds in the home, among them a "Bed for [the] Children," and "a Negro Bed." The latter was for Phebe, a mulatto slave in her mid-twenties. John and Ruhamah relied on Phebe daily as a domestic servant; they tasked her with countless modes of housework, from taking care of their children to cooking meals for the entire family and, occasionally, guests. After all of her work, Phebe would lie down for an uneven rest on the "Negro bed" her master provided her with, worth only half as much as the nearby child's bed. She knew that the Calhoons expected nothing less from her than a lifetime of faithful service and that, by law, she was as much their property as any of the tables, chairs or beds in the household.[39]

For the Calhoons and other families in South Central Pennsylvania, the 1770s were a time of tremendous social upheaval—the culmination of truly revolutionary ideas and beliefs coming to head with the powers that be. The immortal words declaring that "all men are created equal" echoed not as provenance of a past time but rather as a fresh and raw statement, yet to be proved. While some scoffed at the very idea that a peasant was created equal to the largest landholder—or that the Revolution against mighty Britain could even be won—others looked on with hope of a better tomorrow. This optimistic conglomerate included poor farmers and laborers, who stood to benefit the most, alongside a handful of wealthy landholders, who, despite having everything to lose, placed their faith in these enlightenment ideas. Despite these Revolutionary dreams, come 1770, the men and women of Cumberland and York Counties were growing more and more accustomed to slavery in their midst as they sought new futures. Whether they owned slaves themselves, lived and socialized in close proximity with those who did own slaves or merely saw and interacted with slaves or their masters in passing, the ramifications of human bondage touched both young and old—and white and black—in South Central Pennsylvania.

Many miles to the east, a new, concerted push was being made to abolish the institution. Indeed, to the east lay the greater part of colonial Pennsylvania's population and, accordingly so, its political weight. Slavery in Pennsylvania's then capital, Philadelphia, was on the wane. Diseases, no doubt worsened by the close confines of city life, spread rapidly and mercilessly among the enslaved population of Philadelphia. The slave trade boom in the late 1750s had garnered increased backlash toward the institution from the general public. In 1762, many Philadelphians blamed a docked slave ship for prompting a deadly outbreak of some mysterious illness.[40]

Rightly or wrongly, time and again these views became entrenched in popular thought and at times even prompted legislative response. A few years before the 1762 outbreak, a group of anxious Philadelphians had petitioned the legislature, listing "the mischievous [c]onsequences attending the [p]ractice of importing [s]laves into this [p]rovince, and praying a [l]aw to prevent or discourage such [i]mportation for the future." Soon afterward, in 1761, the assembly enacted a ten-pound duty per slave imported into the colony, which apparently pleased both legislators and those in the

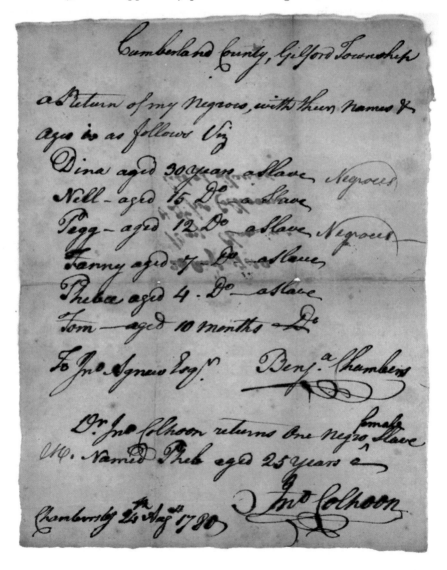

Doctor Jonathan Calhoon's father-in-law, Colonel Benjamin Chambers, owned six slaves in 1780. When the gradual abolition bill was passed, Doctor Calhoon and his father-in-law would share the same document to register their slaves at the then county seat of Carlisle. *Clerk of Courts, Cumberland County Archives.*

Philadelphia area enough so that the duty was raised to twenty pounds per slave in 1773. In Philadelphia and its surrounding counties, the extent of slavery dropped rapidly. After many decades, persistent noise from Quakers had put a dent in the amount of slaveholding Friends. The final blow came in 1774, when the Philadelphia Yearly Meeting banned slaveholding altogether. Other slaveholders in eastern Pennsylvania gradually switched from slave labor to other modes of labor, which they found more convenient. The story was different, however, west of the Susquehanna, in newer communities where slaveholders had made investments more recently.[41]

For all the talk of revolution, liberty, freedom and representation, even amid the Revolution, the number of slaves in Cumberland and York Counties continued to steadily climb. Surviving records show that even as they were engulfed in a war for their own liberty, South Central Pennsylvania slaveholders remained largely unsympathetic to the plight of their slaves. There was to be no great or sudden moral epiphany in this up-and-coming rural society. The idea of labor was central to the region's beginning. It married itself with the core tenants of self-survival, long since embedded in every settler's psyche. Whether it be the possession of labor, by owning slaves or laying claim to indentured servants; or the ability to provide labor for a wage, something the region's poor white population could offer, the labor of the less fortunate was what propelled the plantations, businesses and trade smiths of South Central Pennsylvania to prominence in distant markets across the eastern seaboard.

The act of purchasing of a slave naturally held with it some staying power, as that one payment entitled a master to an entire lifetime of service. From 1765, the number of enslaved men and women in Cumberland County remained level through the end of the decade—from 145 slaves taxed in 1765 to 156 in 1770.[42] However, when more peaceful times rolled around and a pool of white labor reemerged in the early 1770s, the number of slaves took a dramatic decline. By 1775, residents were growing accustomed to a new normal: a minimal amount of slaves alongside a resurgence of indentured servants and other forms of white labor.

The number of indentured servants had more than doubled from around 80 to nearly 200 just five years later. That same time frame had seen Cumberland County's slave population dwindle to 119. Heavily agrarian Antrim township, lying along the Maryland border at the southeastern corner of the county, had long been a stronghold for slavery. Antrim saw its taxable slave population cut in half, from 34 slaves in 1770 to just 17 by 1775. A prime example of this trend is Antrim farmer George Brown, who had been among the largest slaveholders in Cumberland County when he was taxed for ownership of five slaves in 1770. By 1775, he was taxed for only two slaves, and he had added an indentured servant to his labor force.

Brown's feelings about the slaves who toiled for him are unknown—but his actions and those of many of his neighbors indicate a concerted movement away from slave labor. By and large, the names of those who appear as slave owners in 1770 remain on the tax rolls in 1775—meaning that migration by property owners cannot solely account for the drastic drop-off in slaves. Cumberland County slaveholders in all likelihood found ready markets for their slaves farther to the south, in nearby Maryland or even in northern Virginia. Widespread racist attitudes, coupled with a newfound availability of white laborers, combined to erode the use of black labor during the early 1770s.[43]

A sudden reversal came in 1776, when South Central Pennsylvania's landowning class encountered a new shortage of labor. Many of their sons, indentured servants and other poor whites alike marched off to fight in the Revolution. A number of wealthy planters themselves were called off to the war as lieutenants, captains and even colonels, leaving their wives behind to manage the affairs of their properties. These local property holders would have to put aside any stereotypes they entertained about those of African descent in their need for labor. The use of slaves was once again on the upswing in Cumberland County, and within three years, every township in the county had become home to many new slaves.

By 1778, as the Revolution was in full swing, Cumberland County was taxed for 208 slaves—a significant jump from the 119 slaves counted just three years earlier. The full number of enslaved persons was probably closer to 400.[44] Although less is known about the slaves who toiled in York County, in 1779, there were more than 300 slaves taxed county-wide—indicating a total enslaved population exceeding 400 people. The town of York counted over 30 slaves, while farther in the countryside Hamilton Bann township was taxed for more than 50 slaves, Cumberland township for more than 40 and Strabann township for nearly 40.[45]

There is little doubt that many of these slaves had caught wind of the Revolution, and even perhaps the promises of freedom the British had dangled before them. Those who would flee during this time were in all likelihood aware of the conflict, to some extent. It is possible that bondsmen who heard about freedom in British hands sought to reach Philadelphia during its British occupation in 1777–78. Perhaps they were downtrodden by the hypocrisy of their masters, who cried for liberty while they remained in chains—or maybe they simply saw an opportunity to make a run for freedom amid the chaos and turmoil.

York County slaveholder William Alexander, living at Codorus Forge, northeast of York, advertised for the return of his runaway slave in January 1778. Alexander described "a Negroe man, named Jack Johnson, about 35 years of age, 5 feet 8 or 9 inches high, much in the yellowish order; had on when he went away, a small bound felt hat, a new tow shirt, a pair of snuff coloured fustian breeches, lined with check, old stockings and shoes; he is a saucy fellow, and much given to drink. Whoever takes up and secures said Negroe," continued the slaveholder, "so as his master may have him again, shall have the above reward [10 pounds], and reasonable charges if brought home." Johnson, interestingly enough, had run away in September 1777, and only several months after the fact did Alexander finally seek, in print, for his return.[46]

Another bondsman fled York County in January 1778, around the same time that William Alexander finally coughed up the advertisement fee for his long-gone slave. Cornelius Harnett advertised for the return of his mulatto slave Sawney, whom he acknowledged was "well known in this town." Sawney was the epitome of what South Central Pennsylvania slaveholders universally desired—multitalented and skilled, he was, according to Harnett:

> [W]ell built, about 35 years of age, 5 feet 5 inches high, a taylor [sic] by trade, dark complexion, a small face and much fitted with the small pox, had on when he left his master, an old brown Bath coat, osnaburg shirt, thin jacket, linen breeches, yarn stockings, shoes, and an old beaver hat, &c. Whoever apprehends said slave, and delivers him to the Goaler of York-Town, taking his receipt, shall receive Twenty Dollars if taken in the town, or within twenty miles of it, if upwards of twenty miles Thirty Dollars, and all reasonable charges.[47]

Harnett's posting reveals several key realities about slaveholding in South Central Pennsylvania. He, like Alexander, waited a considerable amount of time before spending money to advertise (Alexander waited several months, Harnett three weeks). This tells us that enslaved men and women in South Central Pennsylvania (as they were known to in areas with more historical documentation) often ran away from their masters but, when faced the with the difficult reality of trying to "disappear" amid a population of largely unwelcoming whites, often returned home on their own. Neither Alexander nor Harnett felt a rush to spend money on advertising immediately after their bondsmen had fled, revealing their confidence that their property would return.

Perhaps most suggestive is what these early runaway ads reveal about beliefs in property among South Central Pennsylvania's rural slaveholding class. Both Alexander and Harnett felt entirely justified that Jack Johnson and Sawney were their property. Their ads reveal no moral qualms, no subtle hints of affectionate master-slave relationships. As masters, Alexander and Harnett were the very men standing between the freedom Jack Johnson and Sawney longed for above all else. Their unending view of Johnson and Sawney as property was challenged when the two bondsmen made runs for their freedom. Yet for weeks, they persisted in believing that these two men were still their property, legally and morally, hence there was no immediate need to search for them, much less to expend money to ensure their return.

For Harnett, his admission that Sawney may have fled more than twenty miles from York came only after hesitation. The fact that he posted two separate rewards (a practice adopted by many slave owners), and in the process acknowledged the larger reward as a possibility, reveals him ever so gradually coming to the realization that he had perhaps lost control of what he believed to be his property. The reality of the situation conflicted with his social and cultural understanding of Sawney as a subordinate to him—his purchase, his ownership and his legally obtained labor source was completely and suddenly nullified by Sawney's single act of taking flight. Harnett's advertisement came at the tail end of three weeks in which he was initially filled with confidence at the easy return of his slave, but as the days wore on he would have come to confront the inevitable—the realization that slavery was a much more complex relationship of human emotions and lives than he or other rural whites would ever like to admit.

During this same period in early 1778, other local slaveholders were looking to capitalize on the white labor shortage during the war and sell their slaves while they were in high demand. In Carlisle, tavern keeper Robert White advertised a "*Healthy* stout mulatto *Wench*, 16 years old; she has had the small-pox and measles, can cook, wash, and do most sorts of house-work."[48] A few weeks later, a longtime slave with a family was advertised "to be disposed of." The noticed described a "*Strong* healthy Negro *Man*, has had the small-pox, about 30 years of age, his wife and three children, the eldest of whom is six years: The man has been employed on a farm for some years."[49]

Slave sales among South Central Pennsylvanians were likely more common than surviving records reveal, especially during the colonial years. Few bills of sale remain in archives, and most of our documentation of sales (or the desire to sell) comes from newspaper advertisements. A significant portion, if not a majority, of slave sales were conducted on a local, unadvertised basis between individual slaveholders who discussed terms of sale in their everyday conversations. The parties would typically draw up a notarized bill of sale to make the purchase official, although this nor any type of registration was regulated prior to 1780. By and large, these documents seem to be a hasty and informal procedure usually drawn up on a small sliver of paper. Alongside the signature of the seller and a witness, one such bill from Cumberland County simply read: "Rec^d of Patrick Jack full Satisfaction for a Negro woman (Rachel) bequeath'd to me by my Father at my mothers decease."[50]

The name of Robert Whitehill is written on one of the earliest surviving bills of sale, which dates to November 1770. Whitehill was a resident of East Pennsborough township and an influential Pennsylvania statesman. He had helped to draft the 1776 state constitution, but perhaps most importantly, he was the author of an influential dissent to the Federal Constitution, whose ideas are credited with influencing James Madison and the creation of the Bill of Rights. Yet in 1770, he paid seventy pounds for "one Negro Boy Named Pacoh" who he kept as a slave at least through the next decade.[51] Another surviving bill of sale comes from 1774, when John Kirkpatrick of Letterkenny township sold a "Woman Slave Between a Negro and a Molatta [sic] Named Rhonda Jane" to Joseph Spear of Carlisle, for a sum of eighty pounds.[52]

Communities of free blacks first took root in Philadelphia and soon grew in Harrisburg and even places in the rural countryside of South Central Pennsylvania. Such groups, albeit free by name, were under constant pressure from both rural whites and an unfair legal structure. In 1700, the legislature had set up a separate court system for those of African descent. Under this system, blacks—slave or free—would be tried not by a jury of their peers but by two justices of the peace and "six of the most substantial freeholders of the neighborhood."

Come 1726, the legislature took an even harder line, establishing Pennsylvania's "black code," reminiscent of those farther to the south. When traveling, slaves were required to carry a pass from their master at all times. Further, they were barred from "tippling or drinking in or near any house or shop where strong liquors are sold." The law also gave free blacks reason to be wary. Playing into common stereotypes, the law empowered

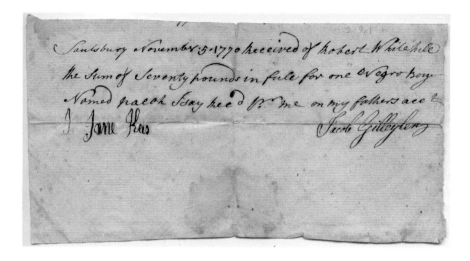

Above: Credited as one of the forces behind the Bill of Rights, East Pennsborough resident Robert Whitehill nonetheless purchased a slave named Pacoh in November 1770. *Cumberland County Historical Society.*

Left: In 1774, Carlisle's Joseph Spear purchased Rhonda Jane, a mulatto woman, from John Kirkpatrick of Letterkenny township, farther down the Cumberland Valley. *Cumberland County Historical Society.*

local officials to seize and "bind out to service" any "free negro fit and able to work" who "neglects" to do so and "loiter[s] and misspend[s] his or her time or wander[s] from place [to place]."

Like most other states at the time, interracial marriage was strongly discouraged, with the consequence that any free black faced possible enslavement or re-enslavement for marrying a white. Free blacks could not interact with slaves, or invite them into their homes, unless they had the slaves' masters' permission. Perhaps most frightening was the provision that allowed children of former slaves to be enslaved until their late twenties. Yet for all it did to separate the races into clear and separate social castes, Pennsylvania's laws concerning African Americans were relatively humane compared to those of Deep South plantation societies. Unlike in many Southern colonies, the punishment for the murder of a slave was the same as the killing of any white man. Also apart from Southern colonies, Pennsylvania had no law prohibiting slaves from learning to read or write.

Despite the hardships the Quaker colony had handed down to African Americans, both slave and free, Pennsylvania would be home to the first legislative abolition of racial slavery in world history.[53] The 1776 state constitutional convention had punted when it came to the peculiar institution, although many of its framers would soon return to finish the task they had left undone. In a public letter dated December 1779, Philadelphian George Bryan reasoned that Pennsylvania was due to receive "[f]rom Europe…the highest honors; for the friends of America, and of human nature, in that part of the world, are astonished to find that a people so enlightened to their own rights, as we are, should remain blind to the case of the poor Africans whom we hold in servitude." He also questioned how any legislator—nay, any Pennsylvanian—could oppose this bill. "Coinciding with, and exactly pursuing the very first words and the main principles of our Constitution, 'that all men are born equally free and independent, and that they have certain natural, inherent and unalienable rights,' a member of the legislature of Pennsylvania must feel himself to be but awkwardly employed in opposing such a design."[54]

Together, Cumberland and York Counties would send fifteen legislators to vote on the gradual abolition bill. York was represented by eight men, four of whom were slaveholders. James Dickson came from Straban township, where he owned some 747 acres and two slaves; David Dunwoodie, from nearby Cumberland township, resided on 504 acres and claimed one slave; Colonel David Kennedy in Hamilton Bann township, with 400 acres and two slaves; and finally Colonel Mathew Dill held one slave on his 353-acre plantation in Manahan township. York's non-slaveholding assemblymen included John Hay, from the town of York; Colonel Henry Schlegel, a farmer in Berwick township; James Leaper, a farmer from Chanceford township; and John Orr of Hopewell township.[55]

Cumberland County was represented in the fall of 1779 by seven men. Three of the seven men—who were among the wealthiest and most influential in the region—were slaveholders. Samuel Culbertson hailed from Letterkenny township, where he owned a 200-acre plantation-farm with four slaves. To the north, in Fermanagh township (modern-day Juniata County), a man named John Harris (not of Harrisburg) owned 374 acres and at least one slave. East Pennsborough township sent Jonathan Hoge, whose surname gave birth to Hogestown. Although Hoge himself was not a slave owner, his brother David owned two slaves on a 328-acre property. From Peters township came William McDowell, a non-slaveholder. Farmer Abraham Smith of Hopewell township and Ephraim Steel, a Carlisle storekeeper, were also non-slaveholders. Finally, Frederick Watts of Rye township (modern-day Perry County) owned 250 acres, a still and a young mulatto woman.[56]

A draft of the abolition bill had been stalled in the legislature since 1778, and amid the turbulent backdrop of the American Revolution, its passage seemed a long shot at best. However, the elections of 1779 had introduced an array of radical legislators, particularly from the Philadelphia area, who would certainly mess with the formula. These radicals included George Bryan himself, one of the earliest proponents of the abolition bill. Bryan revamped the bill, giving it new life. He was forced to make many concessions, however, including the stipulation that children born to an enslaved mother must serve until twenty-eight, a way of compensating slave owners for the charges of "nurture."[57]

Bryan's vision came to fruition on March 1, 1780, when the bill was passed by a vote of thirty-four to twenty-one. Only five members of Cumberland County's delegation voted—Harris, Hoge, Smith, Steel and Watts—but they all voted to abolish the institution. Frederick Watts and John Harris, two of Cumberland County's three slaveholding representatives, thus voted to abolish the very institution they themselves partook in. So, too, did York County's Colonel Mathew Dill and David Dunwoodie, who each owned a slave at the time, yet voted to abolish slavery. The other two slave owners in York's delegation, James Dickson and David Kennedy, were the only two legislators in the region to vote against the gradual abolition. Finally, John Orr, a non-slaveholder, also voted to end the institution. Schlegel, Leaper and Hay—all non-slaveholders—did not vote.[58]

Samuel Culbertson of Letterkenny, one of the largest slaveholding legislators, did not vote against the bill but joined Dickson and Kennedy in signing a dissent that decried passing such a bill during a war. "[W]e approve and are sensible of the humanity and justice of manumitting slaves in time[s] of peace," they wrote, "we cannot think this the proper time." Even if "the time were come when slaves might be safely emancipated, we could not agree to their being made free citizens in so extensive a manner as this law proposes; we think they would have been well satisfied, and the legislature would have sufficiently answered their humane purposes, had these unhappy people been enabled to enjoy the fruits of their labour, and been protected in their lives and property, in the manner white persons are, without giving them the right of voting for, and being voted into offices, intermarrying with white persons, consorting them with their masters, and being witnesses in every respect during the limited time of their servitude, which we fear in some instances may ruin families."[59]

Although it did not free a single slave, the bill was viewed as a smashing success among most abolitionists in the state. They could boast of the first legislative abolition in America, and the first of its kind worldwide. However, any slave born before March 1, 1780, was still facing a life of perpetual servitude. Children of slaves born after that date were required to serve their mother's master until age twenty-eight. In order to enforce these provisions, the law required that slaveholders must register their slaves, and all new slave births, with their respective county clerks. Any slave not registered would be, by default, free.[60]

Yet even this compromise of a law was not a done deal—the radical legislature that had enacted it was largely swept out of office just months later, in October 1780. In Cumberland County, only Hoge, Harris and Culbertson were reelected, and all four new members were slaveholders: John Allison of Antrim, John Andrew of Guilford, William Brown of Armagh and Stephen Duncan of Carlisle. Cumberland County now had six out of seven representatives who were slaveholders, and the only non-slaveholder, Jonathan Hoge, had a slaveholding brother. Out of its eight representatives, York County returned only James Dickson, a slaveholder who had opposed the abolition.[61]

The new assembly members, who might be expected to differ from their predecessors, soon received and read petitions for extensions on when slaveholders could register their slaves and even petitions that went as far as calling for the repeal of the law. Many slaveholders claimed ignorance for neglecting to register their slaves and asked for amendments and extended registration so that their slaves could not go free. Antislavery thinkers throughout Pennsylvania were incredulous at these attempts. "Philotheukos" wrote in the *Pennsylvania Packet* that "[i]gnorance of the law is no excuse in law, because every person ought to know the laws, and it is a plea which can never be disproved...It may be a loss to those individuals, but the injustice to the negroes and discredit to the assembly, would infinitely overbalance any such considerations." Two separate attempts for relaxation of the abolition law were defeated, and so Pennsylvania's slow-moving Bill for the Gradual Abolition of Slavery would stand.[62]

Chapter Five

DEFYING ABOLITION

Disgruntled, though not yet deprived, throughout 1780, the slaveholders of South Central Pennsylvania trudged to their respective county seats, where they would register their slaves. Those residing within the bounds of then gargantuan Cumberland County would have to journey to Carlisle, where they would go before the clerk of the Court of Session. Residents of York County would have to travel to the town of York to list their human chattel. The effort required to register slaves clearly demonstrates that slave owners in South Central Pennsylvania by and large did not have qualms about slaveholding—they would go to troublesome lengths to assert their rights to what they still deemed as their property.

Central to any understanding of South Central Pennsylvanian society in the decades following the Revolution are the intricate series of personal, religious and financial connections formed at both the individual and family levels. Throughout the post-Revolutionary era, travel was conducted on horseback or in a horse-drawn carriage. This mode of transportation often required multiple days and nights, even for locals visiting their county seat. For a man living in East Pennsborough, a seemingly routine trip to the county seat of Carlisle often encompassed a full day affair on horseback, if not more.

A day on horseback to reach one's destination usually meant a night spent away from one's normal abode. For this very reason, as early as 1780 there were countless taverns dotting the main thoroughfares where one might spend the night. However, the formality of a night's stay in the tavern was often cast aside in favor of an opportunity to rekindle an old friendship or a familial tie. South Central Pennsylvanians maintained a complex web of contacts—people they could readily rely upon for hospitality, regardless of how far apart they lived. These webs of connections included many men who never lived in South Central Pennsylvania. However, their business, their travels or their politics had garnered them friends. Benjamin Rush, for instance—a Philadelphia reformer and champion of abolition—had not lived west of the Susquehanna, yet through his efforts at education, he could rely on a wealth of friends who were ready to receive him when he journeyed into the hinterland.

Only in his late thirties, Benjamin Rush had already made waves in the infant nation he called home. Born in 1746 outside of Philadelphia, he was raised by a widowed mother who ran a grocery store in Philadelphia. It was his uncle, Reverend Dr. Samuel Finley, headmaster of Nottingham Academy, who provided Rush's initial education. Rush relentlessly pursued the medical field, and by 1769, he began a medical practice in Philadelphia. With few connections among the elite of Philadelphia, Rush's practice was limited to the poorest elements of the city. Yet steadily working his way up, Rush managed election to the Continental Congress in July 1776, in time to add his name among those signers of the Declaration of Independence.

For a brief time, Rush had been surgeon general of the Middle Department of the Continental Army, but due to in-fighting, he had resigned his commission and returned to private practice.[63] Now a Revolutionary figure with prominence, Rush embarked on a series of endeavors ranging from education to medicine and emancipation. A lifelong abolitionist, in 1773, he wrote of turning down "a thousand guineas a year lately offered to me in Charleston, South Carolina. I am too attached to my own country, this dear province where one owes one's ease only to free and honest toil, to be tempted to exchange it for a country where wealth had been accumulated only by the sweat and blood of Negro slaves."[64] Another time, Rush would pen that "I love even the name of Africa, and never see a Negro slave or freeman without emotions which I seldom feel in the same degree towards my unfortunate fellow creatures of a fairer complexion."[65]

Rush would also be known for his attempts to advance education. He viewed the countryside of Pennsylvania as an experiment ready to be molded. In order for the newly won republic to survive, Rush believed that countryside communities needed to be bursting at the seams with capable, worthy citizens—selfless, devoted and responsible for the common good. The greatest obstacle to the cultivation of selfless young men? Rush blamed a lack of commercialization in rural areas, which he believed brought forth selfishness and incompetency among men. "A college at Carlisle," he wrote in March 1783, "by diffusing the light of science and religion more generally through our society" might "teach...[rural residents] to prefer civil, social, and religious advantages, with a small farm and old land." With this in mind, in 1783, Rush founded Dickinson College in Carlisle, the purpose of his spring 1784 journey there.[66]

Rush crossed the Susquehanna on April 5, and once on its western banks, he wasted no time in paying a visit to "my old friend Dr. Kennady's family on the shore." Continuing westward, he rode on "deep" and "difficult" roads to White's tavern, a small stop midway between Carlisle and the river, where he dined. It was not until evening that he finally trotted into Carlisle. There he met an Irish immigrant named James Pollock, who owned the "large and excellent" tavern on High Street where Rush would spend the night. A guest of Rush's stature naturally meant there would be a bevy of friends ready to receive him, and unsurprisingly, there were. One of Carlisle's foremost citizens, John Montgomery, soon appeared, inviting Rush to spend the night at his Carlisle home. The Philadelphian, fatigued by his travels, declined politely but only with the promise to be Montgomery's guest for breakfast the next morning.[67]

Carlisle seemed to Rush a small mecca of refined civilization amid a vast expanse of rural countryside. "[I]t consists of about 300 houses," Rush later wrote admiringly, "most of which are built of limestone...The inhabitants...are in general an orderly people. Two or three general officers who have served with reputation in our army, four or five lawyers, a regular-bred physician, and a few gentlemen in trade of general knowledge and of fair characters compose the society of the town."[68] Outside of the town, Rush and his consorts drew less inspiration. Scotsman Charles Nisbet, the first president of Dickinson College, cried in a vein Rush himself would have approved, that "ignorance" and "an aversion to labour" on the part of many settlers "prove a dead weight on all schemes of improvement. Hence the

Doctor Benjamin Rush, a physician, education advocate and abolitionist, founded Dickinson College in Carlisle. *Library of Congress.*

lands produce little; most of the ground is in wood or waste; the highways in a state of nature; and the inhabitants, by living so distant from each other, are deprived of the benefit of society, and especially of that emulation which is excited by neighborhood."[69]

Rush was accompanied on this trip by his African slave, William Grubber. A slave-owning abolitionist undeniably reeks of contradiction—however, Rush had purchased Grubber from slavery around 1776, with a comparatively humane intent. He would manumit William after ten years of service, which would allow Rush to recoup Grubber's price and offer William eventual freedom he likely would not have found elsewhere. To Rush, a man who was equally as passionate about temperance as he was about education and emancipation, the drinking and profanity-prone William, or "Billy," was evidence of successful reform. Within two years under his care, Rush later recalled, Billy "was reformed from both these vices" becoming "a sober, moral man and faithful and affectionate Servant." After he was emancipated, their friendly relationship continued until Grubber's death in 1799—Rush wrote that Billy "always made my home his home."[70]

For a man who never eyed "a Negro slave or freeman without emotions," Rush certainly kept strange company during his 1784 visit to Carlisle. James Pollock, who owned the tavern where Rush bedded down for the night, was one of Carlisle's largest slaveholders with seven slaves in 1784. They ranged in age from forty-five-year-old Joe and thirty-five-year-old Venus to girls Jude and Violet, aged nine and six, respectively, and boys Jack and Romeo, aged eight and three. The most recent addition was Dinah, a term slave born in March 1781.[71] Rush also received unflinching hospitality and support from another Carlisle slaveholder, John Montgomery. Alongside Rush, John Montgomery was one of the major backers of Dickinson College. He also owned nine slaves—there was Dinah, who would have been nearing forty around the time of Rush's visit, and then there was Jane, who was in her mid-twenties. They were accompanied by a seventeen-year-old girl, a twelve-year-old girl, and two boys and three girls all aged ten and under.[72]

What Rush thought of his slave-owning hosts went unrecorded—surely he caught glimpses of their large holdings in slaves during his lengthy stay. He nonetheless found James Pollock to be a fascinating man. "My Landlord James Pollock who lives in a good brick house told me that he assisted in cutting down the trees that built the first log house in Carlisle," Rush noted in his diary.[73] Pollock reported another slave birth about a year after Rush's visit, in March 1785, and in his will several years later would bequeath "the Negro Wench Venus" to his wife.[74] The same goes for John Montgomery, who had slaves working in and around his large stone dwelling on the western outskirts of town, known as Happy Retreat. In addition to the eight slaves he registered in 1780, Montgomery would record five slave births during the 1780s: Violet in 1783, Patience and Phillis in 1786, and boys Darby and Harry in 1788.[75]

Unlike Rush, Montgomery was no apologist for slavery. When he no longer needed their service, rather than grant them freedom, Montgomery placed several of his slaves up for sale. He advertised in June 1787 "[a] Strong healthy Negro Wench, and a female Child six months old, the wench is used to house work—Also two negro Boys, one about six and the other about four years old."[76] This approach did not change, even as mortality called upon him—Montgomery willed that most of his property should be sold off "Except my negro man Thomas and my waggon [*sic*] and horses which I allow to be kept for the use of the family until the next spring."[77]

After attending services the following morning, Rush and William made their way to Happy Retreat. Alongside them were roughly a dozen or so men who could call themselves trustees of the infant Dickinson College and a few others, all gathering within for a meal attended only by the highest of society. "Our dinner was plentiful," recorded a somewhat surprised Rush, "elegant & as well attended as any dinner I ever was at in a Gentleman's house in Philadelphia." Much like the town itself, Montgomery and his family impressed Rush with sophistication and class amid a remote region hundreds of miles outside of Philadelphia. Rush took particular note of his associate's wife, Sarah Montgomery, and one of his daughters, whom he considered "sensible well bred women."[78] Rush spent several more days in Carlisle organizing the infant college, repeatedly dining at either Pollock's or Montgomery's. Toward the end of his visit, he journeyed to Colonel Robert Magaw's home on the square for tea. Magaw, a lawyer, Revolutionary war veteran and trustee of Dickinson College, also owned a young male slave named Sip.[79] For all his disdain of slavery, Rush seemed content to remain mum on the talk of abolition and instead enjoy the education and "civility" of Carlisle's elite society.

On April 9, Rush bade farewell to his friends in Carlisle and set off with William for Philadelphia. Heading south over the mountains, Rush and William endured an "extremely disagreeable" daylong ride. It was cold, and the winding, mountainous roads "in many places were covered w[ith] [s]now above a foot deep." Nearing York, Rush was greeted by "about a dozen…Gentlemen" of the town, a few miles outside, who accompanied him on his ride in. Arriving at dusk, Rush found lodging with his "good friend and kinsman" Archibald McClean, a cousin. McClean, the prothonotary of York County, owned three slaves.[80]

Rush had just departed the company of another of his York County connections, Colonel Robert McPherson. The McPhersons had been among the first white settlers along Marsh Creek, a short way west of what later became Gettysburg. Robert McPherson had been sent east to Chester County for his education, but he returned to the Gettysburg area, where he had property in Cumberland township. Around the time of Rush's visit, the colonel had 828 acres, which were worked by eleven slaves. As a prominent local citizen and legislator, McPherson provided valuable support to Rush. He was known to his friends and neighbors as a soldier and had been elected to a variety of offices including auditor, commissioner, sheriff and assemblyman from the 1750s on and off through the 1780s. McPherson maintained a close relationship with Benjamin Rush and was one of the assemblymen who helped push forward the charter for Dickinson College, of which he was a trustee.[81]

The South Central Pennsylvania Benjamin Rush saw in 1784 was an incredibly divided and divergent area. Despite the passage of the gradual abolition act, rich and poor alike were opting to ignore the light at the end of the tunnel for slave children who were to one day be free and continued to treat slaves and their post-abolition offspring as human chattel, one in the same. White residents were also eager to point fingers when it came to poverty among new communities of free blacks, attributing it to racial inferiority rather than considering the setbacks incurred by slavery.[82]

Under the pain of losing their bondsmen and women, slaveholders would often travel long distances to appear before county clerks and register their slaves. In 1780, following passage of the gradual abolition act, masters were required to register all slaves currently held with their names, gender, age and often even skin color. Amendments to the law passed in 1788 to fill loopholes mandated the registration of any term-slave children (those who were to be free at age twenty-eight) born to a slave mother after March 1, 1780. It also made it illegal for a slaveholder to separate families by selling members of the same family more than ten miles away.[83]

In these registrations, slaveholders would have an incentive to divulge accurate and complete information, giving the names, ages and racial background of their slaves. The surviving slave registries, therefore, offer a trove of rich and detailed information about slaves and their masters and an unprecedented glimpse into South Central Pennsylvanian slavery.

Either in person or by attorney, slave owners were mandated to deliver this information to their county clerks, who were then entitled by law to a two-dollar fee per slave registered.[84]

The law was at best an inconvenience to slaveholders in South Central Pennsylvania, who did not see freeing their slaves as a viable option. For men such as Colonel Mathew Dill and David Dunwoodie, two slaveholding representatives from York County who nonetheless voted to abolish the institution, their reactions probably went as far as chafing at the inconvenience of registering their slaves. Others, however, who had never supported the law and saw no need to apologize for slavery, were not as tranquil.

Carlisle's George Stevenson was outraged at the law when he went to register his three slaves in 1780 and ended up recording his reaction on the same parchment with which he registered his slaves. He lashed out at what he deemed a "useless Act of the General Assembly" and angrily mocked Cumberland County's clerk of the Court of Session, John Agnew, chiding, "I hope he will be paid Six Dollars, which is the only good [t]hing in the Act, for it will help to pay his Tax."[85] Shippensburg merchant Francis Campbell echoed Stevenson some eight years later, scribbling on a registration for two slave births that the law "is a[ttended] with some difficultys [sic] which are so surprising, that Gentlemen who esteem themselves men of sense and wish to be in high reputat[ion] with their neighbours should spend time and load the Inhabitants with Expenses in making such frivolous Laws as respect the matter in hand."[86]

The slave registries reveal that, for decades, tax collectors had been using shortcuts in their tallies of slaves. By rule of thumb, tax collectors did not tax slave children and any other slaves whom they deemed should not be taxed. Take for instance Henry Pawling, an Antrim slaveholder who was taxed for four slaves in 1780, the very same year he registered thirteen slaves. Pawling held seven slaves who were eighteen and older and six under eighteen— three fifteen-year-old females, a four-year-old boy, a two-year-old girl and a one-year-old boy.[87] Based on a 1763 inventory of the Pawling plantation done upon his father's death, many of the slaves registered in 1780 belonged to his father some seventeen years earlier. For instance, a "negroe man Named Secar" is listed in 1763, likely a phonetic interpretation of the name "Cesar," who in 1780 was a fifty-six-year-old slave at the Pawling plantation. Also there was "a Malatto boy Named Sam" who appears in the 1780 registration as thirty-four-year-old mulatto Sam. The same goes for "a Malatto Girl Cate" who in 1780 is listed as thirty-two-year-old Cate. Also there are two "boys" named James and Tom, who are undoubtedly

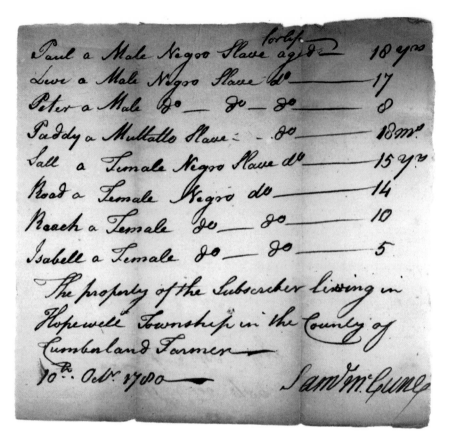

In October 1780, Hopewell township farmer Samuel McCune registered eight slaves, ranging from eighteen years to eighteen months old. *Clerk of Courts, Cumberland County Archives.*

the twenty-six-year-old Tom and twenty-one-year-old Jim listed in 1780.[88] Cesar, Sam, Cate, Tom and Jim had spent their entire lives thus far toiling for two generations of Pawling family patriarchs, and despite the gradual abolition, as far as Henry Pawling was concerned, they would continue to labor the rest of their lives for him and then for his children.

Without the surviving slave registrations, tax records would conceal much of the true dimensions of slave labor on the Pawling plantation and elsewhere. In 1782, a state law was passed clarifying that "all negro and mulatto slaves above the age of twelve" were to be taxed.[89] However, this had clearly been a common practice for some time. In 1769, Antrim's Thomas Poe was taxed for one slave. Yet in an estate inventory done shortly afterward, Poe's holdings show "one Negro Man" and "one Molatto Boy."[90]

Also revealing is the case of Carlisle slaveholder Charles Pattison, who in 1770 was taxed for only one slave, yet a 1771 estate inventory listed "1 Negro Woman & Child" along with three other "boys."[91] Slavery goes far beyond the dimensions of active labor that tax collectors sought to record. Even an infant slave, incapable as yet of doing any work, was still born into a life of bondage. To understand and appreciate the full human impact of slavery, the entire body of enslaved persons working, living and growing up amid the South Central Pennsylvania economy must be taken into consideration. The existence of the slave registry provides exactly that—a wide, all-encompassing scope of slavery in Cumberland County.

There were no fewer than 695 slaves within Cumberland County in 1780. This count includes municipalities within the modern-day borders of Cumberland and Franklin Counties, encompassing the Cumberland Valley, but excludes townships north of the mountains, in what later became Perry, Juniata and Mifflin Counties. At the time, those regions were lopped in under the broad banner of Cumberland County, and if included, they would bring the county-wide total to 775 slaves. Scarcely had the slave registry begun when in 1784 the lines were redrawn and Franklin was formed as a separate county unto itself. Of the 695 slaves included within those borders

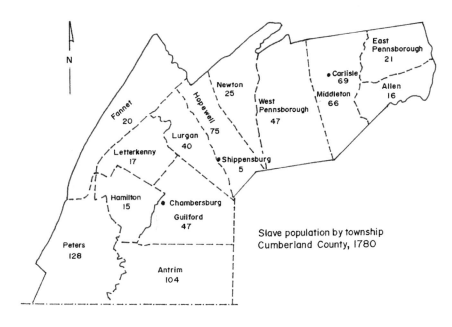

Slave registrations in Cumberland County, 1780. *Map by John Heiser.*

in 1780, 371 were within the future limits of Franklin County and 324 in what remained Cumberland County.[92]

In the Cumberland County of 1780, the average age of a bondsmen was seventeen. The oldest recorded slave was a seventy-year-old man named Sharper, who belonged to James Galbreath of East Pennsborough. Galbreath also owned the oldest female slave registered, sixty-year-old Chloe. There was a nearly even divide between males and females, and among females, nearly 200 were of child-bearing age. Racially, 89 slaves were identified as mulattoes, or having a mixed lineage. Antrim township led the entire county with 25 slaves identified as mulattoes; neighboring Peters had 19, and another rural township, West Pennsborough, counted 7. The more urban setting of Carlisle numbered 10 mulattoes. Peters township, as it had since the 1760s, remained one of the largest slaveholding municipalities, registering some 128 slaves. Antrim followed close behind with 104, and beyond those two were another tier of large slaveholding townships comprising Hopewell (80), Middleton (66), West Pennsborough (47), Guilford (47) and Lurgan (40). Most other valley townships averaged around 20 slaves.

Popular names for female slaves included Pegg, Bett or Betty, Hannah, Dinah, Fanny, Nance or Nancy, Violet, Jude and Lucy or Luce. Common male names included Ben, Bob, Cato, Dick, Pomp or Pompey, Sampson, Tim and Tom. Others invoked more classical themes. Eight males were registered under the name Cesar and another eight females under the name Venus. There were several males named Paris, one named Prince, another under the name Hercules and one named Julius. For females, some included Prudence, Patience and Pleasant. Five males bore the name of "Sambo."[93]

Within Cumberland County, about 71 percent of the slaves registered belonged to farmers and millers. Many owned plantations spanning several hundred acres, growing any number of crops; others operated gristmills instead of or often in addition to traditional farming activities. Although some small farms employed slave labor, the weight of agricultural slavery belonged to the larger landholders. There were 201 self-identified farmers and millers who registered nearly 500 slaves among themselves in 1780. Of the 201 slave owners, roughly 70 laid claim to three or more slaves. Around 8 percent of slaves were in the hands of masters who had distinguished themselves enough to bear titles such as esquire, general, colonel, captain and even sheriff and reverend. Five slaves called reverends their master in 1780: Reverend John King of Peters township owned twenty-five-year-old Sue and two-year-old Luce. Samuel Dougal of Fannett claimed twenty-five-year-old Chloe, Thomas McPherran of Peters claimed fifteen-year-old Dolly

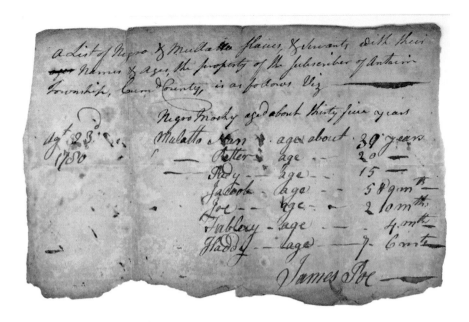

When James Poe's father died in 1770, he rose to the head of one Antrim's many slaveholding families. As he fought in the Revolution, Poe increased his slaveholdings to eight bondsmen, which he registered in 1780. *Clerk of Courts, Cumberland County Archives.*

and James Long of Antrim had twelve-year-old Nell. Five slaves belonged to doctors, the largest slaveholding doctor being Richard Brownson of Peters township, with 3 slaves. Doctors Robert Henry of Hopewell township and Jonathan Calhoon in Chambersburg each owned 1 slave. Some 7 percent of slaves belonged to more trade-oriented masters, such as carpenters, blacksmiths, masons, tanners, tailors, tobacconists and powder makers. Another 3 percent had masters who were in regular business with the public—from merchants and shopkeepers to bakers to tavern keepers. No less than 14 slaves found themselves working for tavern keepers in 1780.[94]

Unfortunately, the same depth of records does not survive for York County. The best available documentation lies in a 1783 tax, in which tax collectors kept note of how many non-taxed slave children under age twelve resided in the county. York County totaled 584 slaves, and out of those, 398 were above twelve years of age, while 186 were under. Slave populations were fairly spread out compared to Cumberland County. The northern stretch of the county, bordering Cumberland, had very small slave populations, due in part to the heavy Quaker populations they held. The town of York counted 61 slaves in 1783, and outside of the town the next tier of slaveholding

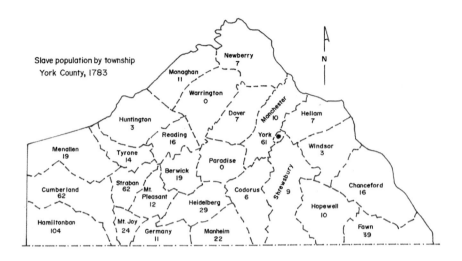

Slaves in York County, 1783. At the time, York County still encompassed modern-day Adams County. *Map by John Heiser.*

townships was found along the southern border, in Fawn (39), Manheim (22) and Heidelberg (29) townships. In what was destined to become Adams County, slavery was concentrated around the centrally located town of Gettysburg (Cumberland and Straban townships each counted 62 slaves), while in the southwestern corner, Hamiltonbann township led the entire county with 104 slaves.[95]

All things considered, by the mid-1780s there were well over one thousand slaves toiling in the modern counties of Cumberland, Franklin, Adams and York. Slaves made up a significant portion of the workforce throughout the late eighteenth and early nineteenth centuries. Their presence incited jealousy and competition anxiety from poor white laborers, who even more so feared for their own place in society with a looming emancipation. They were not too far-fetched with their concerns—Benjamin Rush gleefully told a friend in 1785 that emancipated slaves in Philadelphia "are in general more industrious and orderly than the lowest class of white people."[96]

Rush, however, was far removed from the day-to-day scene in rural South Central Pennsylvania, where a different type of social fabric was being woven. Slaves were employed in nearly every profession, and in their daily lives they recurrently toiled for the benefit of white masters—a fact that was not soon lost on white property holders. This class of white citizens, with a few exceptions, by and large did not wish or desire to see emancipation. Neither did laboring-class whites, who would have to question their place against independent, free blacks. In part because of these very economic and social concerns, social pressure to do away with slavery did not impact the slaveholders in South Central Pennsylvania as it had in the eastern parts of the state. In Cumberland County, the class of largely Presbyterian slaveholders received little pressure from the pulpit to cut ties with the institution, as Quakers had. And with rural whites in no rush to have free African Americans entering the labor force, there was no popular current to ride in the cause of emancipation.[97]

Therefore, it is difficult to say what kind of thoughtful discussion was given to issues of bondage and race. Some hints can be gleaned from a weekly paper entitled the *Carlisle Gazette and the Western Repository of Knowledge*, which began publication in 1785. For the next several decades, the pages of the *Gazette*, alongside other local papers, would be peppered with references to slavery. What discussions were had about the morals of the institution have gone largely unrecorded amid the annals of history, and considering what the *Gazette* printed, it is unlikely that there were many at all.

The *Gazette* occasionally offered racially charged anecdotes, which they apparently hoped would produce a chuckle among the literate populace. One of these "anecdotes" depicted an elderly man calling his lifelong slave "Cato" to his deathbed. The master promised Cato that "he would do him a very great honour before he would die." Cato, assuming his master was alluding to a monetary reward, "thanked him kindly in the usual homely style, and hoped that massa would live long." The paper chronicled the ensuing dialogue between the two, beginning with the master's statement:

> *"I intend, Cato, said the dying master, to put a clause in my will that shall entitle you to be buried in the family vault." "Ah! massa, returns Cato, me no like that, ten pounds would be better to Cato; he no care where he be buried." "But you fool continues the master, would it not be a great honour to you!"—"Honour, massa! me no study honour! interjects the slave, but suppose massa, we should both be buried in one vault, and the devil come looking for massa in the dark, he might take away poor negar man in mistake, and that would neither be honor or profit for Cato."*[98]

Cato was a fairly common name given to slaves across the region, and for

Complying with the 1788 law, in August 1789, Newton township farmer James Nicholson registered the births of two mulatto term slaves, Sall (1783) and Turner (1786). *Cumberland County Historical Society.*

many the scenario of a faithful slave at his master's bedside may have seemed like a reality to many readers. How much humor, debate or disgruntlement these anecdotes—equally stinging to all parties—maintained is lost to history. The *Gazette* did run at least one more, some three years later. It once again involved a slave, this time being asked what color he believed the devil to be. "Why, replied the African, the white men paint him black, we say he is white; but from his great age, and being called Old Nick, I should suppose him grey."[99]

Within the walls of Rush's Dickinson College, however, discussions on race and bondage took deeper consideration amid the backdrop of rural slavery. The Belles Lettres Society, which routinely held debates on political and moral topics, discussed slavery frequently. Record of their debates about slavery date back to the summer of 1786. Then, the question proposed for debate was "Whether it is lawful for Americans to enslave for life, those who have never forfeited their Lives or Liberties, to the States." Having witnessed slavery all around them, both in the streets of Carlisle and the surrounding countryside, a majority of the group's members decided it was not lawful.[100]

The society returned to the discussion a year later, when it was decided that "each member should prepare a Composition on the Subject of Slavery."[101] Although the compositions do not survive, bondage remained an issue upon which Dickinson's constant influx of local and out-of-state students conversed with frequency and alacrity. Perhaps the most memorable of these discussions came some two years later, in July 1789. The question before the scholars asked if "individual Slaveholders in America in their Capacity as Masters [are] justifiable in still retaining their Negroes in Slavery in the present Situation of American Affairs or not." Two students, Joseph S. Galbreath and Francis Dunlavy, entered into a lengthy and fiery debate.

Galbreath opened in the affirmative, and although the exact content of his arguments are lost to history, we can imagine he spoke of anything from property rights, to racial inferiority or even biblical justification of slavery in making his case. Dunlavy, a Winchester, Virginia native, might have been expected to agree, considering he hailed from a slaveholding state. Yet it was that very reality that caused Dunlavy to respond "with great Warmth…on the Negative." We know not what Dunlavy said that afternoon, but we do know what he wrote and spoke about slavery in the years to follow.

Francis Dunlavy was destined to move west, into what was then the Northwestern Territory. Elected to the territorial legislature, by 1802 he had been elected to the convention devising a constitution for the newly forming state of Ohio. At Ohio's constitutional convention, Dunlavy strenuously opposed multiple attempts to allow slavery in the state's constitution and even went as far to propose black suffrage and equal political rights regardless of color. Although he failed, Dunlavy was far ahead of his times in terms of racial justice, and he went on to serve as a state senator and later a judge.

A glimpse into his future leaves little doubt as to what Francis Dunlavy must have said on that July 1789 day in Carlisle. His contemporaries knew him to reference his birth in a slave state, and after having witnessed slavery all his childhood, he only "looked with abhorrence on every system of human bondage." Perhaps that day he alluded with disgust to the signs of slavery outside the walls of Dickinson College. If Galbreath made any mention of racial inferiority, we can imagine how fiercely and personally Dunlavy may have replied. Unlike most meetings of the Belles Lettres Society, this debate was particularly polarizing and unendingly long. The minutes of the society record that "they had both entered largely into the Subject which took up above…one hour & a half & as singing School was to be held…precisely at 4

Virginia native and abolitionist Francis Dunlavy walked the streets of Carlisle during the 1780s and '90s while the town was still home to more than seventy slaves. *Warren County Historical Society, Lebanon, Ohio.*

oClock it was thought proper to postpone the [r]emainder of the arguments till the next Session."[102]

Throughout the following decades, incoming members of the society debated everything from the abolition of slavery to the treatment of Native Americans. A July 1794 debate was one of the many to propose the statement "Negro Slavery ought to be abolished." Among the ranks of the society on this particular day was Roger Brooke Taney, who would graduate from Dickinson the following year. A future chief justice of the Supreme Court, Taney was the very man who in 1857 would hand down the infamous Dred Scott ruling on slavery. Sixty-some years earlier, on this July day, Taney sided on the negative, believing slavery should not be abolished, although the group decided otherwise by a majority at their next meeting.[103]

In their pursuit of reason-based answers, the students who belonged to the Belles Lettres Society would have read many of the available works on bondage and race to prepare their arguments. If they had turned to Benjamin Rush's works, they would have stumbled upon his vision for civilizing the enslaved populace. Rush promised that by educating freed slaves "in the higher branches of science, and in all the useful parts of learning, and in the precepts of religion and morality, we shall not only do away with the reproach and calumny so unjustly lavished upon us, but confound the enemies of truth by evincing that the unhappy sons of Africa, in spite of the degrading influence of slavery, are in no wise inferior to the more fortunate inhabitants of Europe and America."[104]

Yet if the students picked up Edward Long's 1774 *History of Jamaica*, they would have been prodded to consider race in their estimations of whether bondage was just or unjust. Long's *History* spoke a great deal about skin color, attributing it to "the dark membrane which communicates that black colour to their skins...which does not alter by transportation into other climates, and which they never lose, except by such diseases, or casualties, as destroy the texture of it." As proof of racial inequality, Long provided that "the Blacks born here, to the third and fourth generation, are not at all different in colour form those Negroes who are brought directly from Africa."[105] If they disagreed with Long's work on race, students probably gravitated toward that of their college's founder, who believed that darker skin colors were a temporary phenomenon. "I am now preparing a paper," Rush wrote to Thomas Jefferson in 1797, "in which I have attempted to prove that the black color...of the Negroes is the effect of a disease in the skin of a leprous kind."[106]

A future chief justice of the U.S. Supreme Court, Roger Taney oversaw the infamous Dred Scott ruling in 1857, at the time a major legal victory for the slaveholding interests. *Library of Congress.*

For all that had transpired, several years removed from the success of the gradual abolition, slaveholders in Cumberland, Franklin and York Counties showed no signs of moral epiphany. Nay, if anything, slaveholders voiced disgruntlement at the trouble to register their bondsmen and women. For the slaves born prior to March 1, 1780, their masters, together with the commonwealth of Pennsylvania, had left no light at the end of the tunnel. Indeed, the gradual abolition meant little to them, except as a crushing blow of disappointment. The horizon dawned only slightly brighter for their children, born after the law's passage, who would still endure multitudes of hardship and an uphill battle to claim the freedom that was rightfully theirs at age twenty-eight. Slavery may have been on the way out elsewhere, but in South Central Pennsylvania, the chains of bondage were as tight as they had ever been.

Chapter Six

"THE GENERAL PRESSURE OF THE TIMES"

Freedom's Fetters and Freedom Seekers

*To the inhabitants of the borough of York and its vicinity
to the distance of 10 miles.*

*YOU are hereby notified, that such as you have negroes or people of colour, to keep
them at home under strict discipline and watch; so as they may be under your eye
at all times. You are not to let them come into the borough of York on any pretence
[sic] whatever without a written pass, and to whom his errand is directed, and
not to converse with any person, and that they depart out of said borough at least
one hour before sun down, on pain of being imprisoned or at the risk of their
lives. And it is required that all free negroes or people of colour in said borough or
its vicinity, to get a pass from a Justice of the Peace, in order that they may not be
restrained from their daily labour.*[107]

The civic leaders of York made the difficulties faced by African
Americans painfully clear in their 1803 public ordinance. A little
over a decade earlier, the first federal census had counted some 1,300
free blacks living in Cumberland, Franklin and York Counties. Combined
with the slave population, the three counties were home to 2,368 African
Americans. For blacks in South Central Pennsylvania, freedom did not
necessarily mean economic freedom. As the census shows, many of those
same free blacks still lived on plantations worked by slaves and owned and
run by slaveholders. They may have had familial connections to some
of the slaves, but many more found the racial attitudes of those around

them too difficult to make a living. Slaveholder Richard Beard of Peters township was listed with seven free blacks and seven slaves on his property. For these seven men and women, "freedom" was a very limited concept that had them living beside and much like slaves.

There were only thirteen black heads of household in 1790—eight in Franklin County, four in Cumberland and one in York. Examples include a Franklin County man listed as "Black George," who had four other free African Americans living with him; another, Jim, a mulatto, had seven free blacks in his house, similar to a "yellow" woman named Moriah who had two other freed persons living with her. In Cumberland County, black heads of household varied from Thomas Lookwell, who lived with three other free blacks, to "Black Peter," who lived alone. In York, Benjamin Edmiston resided with two other freed persons.[108] Tangible differences between freedom and slavery for blacks around the turn of the century would have been hard to discern to an observing eye, just as it would have been to both those who toiled and those who benefited. This state of muddled freedom was satisfactory to white masters, who still enjoyed the benefits of black labor.

Jube Harris, a free African American who worked in a Carlisle blacksmith shop, was injured on the job. Confined to his home for two months and devoid of a wage, Harris was still unable to work and was "cast" into the county jail for indebtedness. Harris recovered while in jail, but by then, the law and debt prevented him from returning to work.[109] Others, like Francis Smith of Carlisle, a "coloured man & labourer," struggled to find any work, and ended up insolvent in 1818.[110]

Freeman Richard Sanders of Cumberland County had "a wife and three small children" along with his mother-in-law to support. Much like Francis Smith, Sanders encountered what he termed a "difficulty to procure money" and petitioned the county for relief. Among his reported possessions, Sanders listed merely "1 Bed & bedding together with other household furniture not exceeding in the whole...fifteen dollars."[111] Not dissimilar was the case of Samuel Howard in 1826. When his wife became sick for an extended period, Howard was left "to maintain her in that situation with five children." Like so many other free blacks, Howard was forced to file for relief.[112] Thomas Early, another free black in Cumberland County, told the court in 1825 that his white creditors "did not allow him sufficient time to earn the requisite sums to pay them."[113]

Most other freemen were faced with the same situation. John Coleman, a weaver, had a wife and "three small children," but his wife went blind and was confined almost entirely to bed. Like so many others, Coleman was thrown into jail for one of the debts he accumulated during this time. During the past two years, he had "not had sufficient employment at his business, and when he had, [he] was often obliged to leave his work on account of the sickness of his wife, and the care of his children, and finally, the general pressure of the times."[114] Life did not get better for John Coleman. Only four years later he returned, seeking relief once again. With his wife blind and "incapable [of] rendering any aid," Coleman still could not strike a balance between employment and raising a family.[115]

There was little sympathy for the struggles of the local African American community. If they were not thrown in jail for debt, they might be remanded to the poorhouse. In 1814, the Cumberland County poorhouse listed seven free blacks among its thirty-four residents, in addition to an infant mulatto child, named Betsey. A 113-year-old man named Sharper was accompanied by a 101-year-old woman named Chloe—very likely the same Sharper and Chloe who were registered as slaves in 1780 by James Galbreath of East Pennsborough. Evidently after gaining their freedom, they had struggled like many others to gain an economic foothold and ended up spending their final days in the poorhouse. There were others, however—from an 18-year-old female to a 70-year-old female, a bed-ridden man and a blind, 73-year-old man.[116]

Altogether, it was not an inspiring portrait. A vast number of free blacks lived and worked on plantations or iron forges owned by white men, either in lieu of or in addition to legally bound slaves. With little legal protections, those of African descent might at any time be thrown into county jails on mere suspicion of being fugitive slaves. The York jailer advertised in early 1789 "a Negro man, who calls himself Henry Horte, about 24 years of age…he is very smart and [an] expert in…walking on his hands, and says he has no master. The owner, if any, is desired to come within four weeks from this date, otherwise he will be sold for his fees."[117]

For all the hardships endured by free blacks, hundreds more remained in bondage for decades after the gradual abolition. It is impossible to understate the multitude of connections between freemen and slaves. Most interactions were by word of mouth and thus lost to history, but contributions made by free blacks in future years on the Underground Railroad suggest a close and helping relationship for the most part. An 1809 bill of sale from York widow Jennet Grier reveals that her slave, Phyllis Harris, was sold for twenty dollars to free black John Madison. It is impossible to say for sure, but considering both the extremely low price and the verbiage of the document, it seems

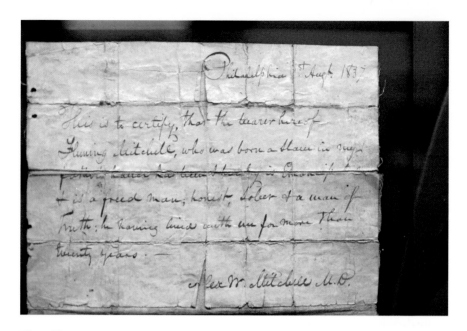

These "free papers" were carried by Fleming Mitchell, a slave to Dr. Alex W. Mitchell of Philadelphia. One of the last slaves in Philadelphia, this 1837 emancipation document from Dr. Mitchell declares Fleming "a freed man; honest, sober & a man of truth; he having lived with me for more than twenty years." Throughout Pennsylvania, men and women of African descent carried papers similar to this, a testament to the need to constantly clarify and prove their freedom. *Fort Hunter.*

likely that the sale was arranged for Phyllis's benefit, possibly as a prelude to her marriage to Madison.[118]

Few slaves fared as well as Phyllis Harris. Most bondsmen faced masters who viewed and treated them solely as property. Many could look forward to nothing but long hours of work, be it on a farm, at an iron forge or in a trade shop. Others might fare better if they were household servants. Domestic servants were especially at high demand in places such as Carlisle and York, county seats that both had their fair share of wealthy lawyers and prominent officers living in town. One such lawyer, James Hamilton of Carlisle, would embark on a decade-plus quest to purchase a slave in the late 1790s.

For whatever reason, Hamilton seems to have decided from the very beginning to purchase a slave from the Philadelphia market rather than locally. He had several agents scour the city for a suitable slave, regularly reporting back to him. One of his associates, William Parker, informed him in October 1811 that he had "[c]alled at the House where the Black Boy was for sale, his master informed me he was then in the Country at his Fathers a few miles from the City, but that he expected him home in the course of a week. I called a second time but he had not returned, when he dose [*sic*], he will let me know, he has about 8 years to serve, his price for him is $140." Alongside the expected purchase of a human being was an answer to Hamilton's desire for "a Bag or two of fine Coffee."[119]

Yet Hamilton's purchase of this particular boy fell through. "The Negro Boy which I last wrote you about," Parker informed him, "was sold during my stay in the Country to a person in Lancaster." Not to despair, Parker attempted to console his friend: "I have been this morning with Mr. Joshua Humphrey, of this City, who advertises a Black Boy for sale, who has between 11 & 12 years to serve, he says he is an excellent waiter, and understands taking Care of Horses and driving a Carriage—he is between 15 & 16 years of age—his price is $150—Should the above meet your approbation you can send... a check by the return mail."[120]

Hamilton replied back eagerly with a check, and Parker triumphantly informed the Carlisle lawyer of his acquisition. Speaking of the boy, Parker penned, "He is now ready and will be sent forward by the first wagon going your way, that will take charge of him—I have had the Indenture made out in the usual way and in your name—which with the receipt for the amount paid at Mr. Humphrey shall be forwarded your way by some safe hand."[121] After receiving confirmation, however, Hamilton appears to have had some doubts about Humphrey's reasons for selling the boy. "In a former letter I gave you a sketch of the Negro Boys Character," Parker replied, trying to soothe his client's nerves, "as I received it from his Master Mr. Joshua Humphreys a Gentlemen of respectability and voracity, his reasons for disposing of the Boy are these, That once when he was sent to Market he appropriated...[money] to buy Cakes for himself out of the Money that was given to him, but he believes him to be perfectly honest otherwise, that he is in no way given to Liquor or telling falsehoods."

Parker expressed his confidence that "by his being sent into the Country, he will become a valuable servant and grow up strictly honest." He repeated to Hamilton that the boy "has waited on Tables, and been entrusted with the Key" to "where the Liquor was, and that in no Instance he was found to use any of it. He is capable of taking care of Horses and driving a Carriage well, which he has done for the last 2 years, to the entire satisfaction of Mr. Humphreys." He also explained that he was meeting with trouble in sending the young boy out to Carlisle. "If you know of any person from Carlisle now in this City...perhaps I may prevail on them to take him up in the stage, as his servant, which I suppose will cost but half fare—and at this inclement season he would have more inducements to run away if he was so dispared by sending him by waggon [*sic*]."[122]

Parker was in luck, and within a week he had stumbled across James Gray Leiper, a Dickinson College student who "kindly offered his services to take the black Boy Luke under his care for you—the expenses I have paid, and shall forward you a statement." Sometime in early January, the young college student delivered Luke to James Hamilton. The Carlisle esquire was evidently pleased, and on the back of a January 31, 1812 letter, his associate Parker detailed the list of expenditures in buying Luke. The process began with a $190 payment from Hamilton. Parker then explained that $3 was employed "for Horse hire &c. to go to Mr. Joshua Humphreys on the Lancaster Road to have the Black Boy purchased to go in the State to Carlisle," $10 in expenses to James Leiper for sending Luke to Carlisle, another $1 for the indenture form, $150 for the actual purchase of Luke and other expenses such as taxes. In the end, Parker owed Hamilton a small balance due of $1.93, which he hoped his brother would soon deliver in person.[123]

Why Hamilton insisted on purchasing a slave from Philadelphia is a mystery. There was no shortage of slave labor available in his home town of Carlisle, and the neighboring villages and countryside. Spanning from its beginnings in 1785, the *Carlisle Gazette* was filled with slave advertisements on a regular basis.

> *TO BE SOLD*
> *A strong healthy Negro Wench,*
> *about twenty-one years of age,*
> *who is sober and honest. Enquire of*
> *the printers.   Aug. 29, 1785.*[124]

> *To be Sold,*
> *Two Negro Men and two Ne-*
> *-gro Women*
> *Enquire of the Printer.*[125]

Other advertisements might include a detailed description of the slaves available—often applying cruder language—such as this York County slaveholder who sought to "dispose" of his slaves in 1789: "To be sold, two stout healthy Negroe Men and a Wench; one is a young lad, about 21 years old; the other two not exceeding 32 years each: They were brought up

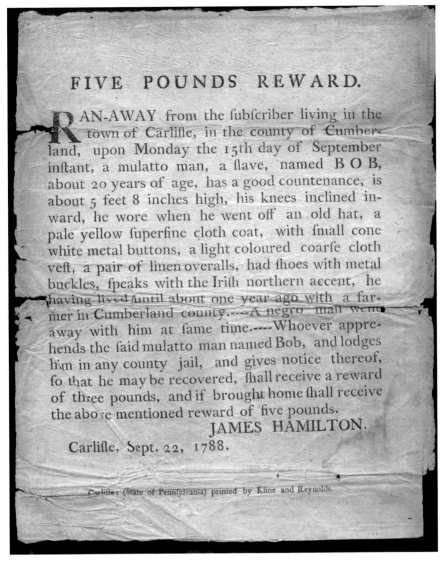

FIVE POUNDS REWARD.

RAN-AWAY from the fubfcriber living in the town of Carlifle, in the county of Cumberland, upon Monday the 15th day of September inftant, a mulatto man, a flave, named B O B, about 20 years of age, has a good countenance, is about 5 feet 8 inches high, his knees inclined inward, he wore when he went off an old hat, a pale yellow fuperfine cloth coat, with fmall cone white metal buttons, a light coloured coarfe cloth veft, a pair of linen overalls, had fhoes with metal buckles, fpeaks with the Irifh northern accent, he having lived until about one year ago with a farmer in Cumberland county.----A negro man went away with him at fame time.-----Whoever apprehends the faid mulatto man named Bob, and lodges him in any county jail, and gives notice thereof, fo that he may be recovered, fhall receive a reward of three pounds, and if brought home fhall receive the above mentioned reward of five pounds.

JAMES HAMILTON.

Carlifle, Sept. 22, 1788.

Carlifle: (State of Pennfylvania) printed by Kline and Reynolds.

In 1788, the publishers of the *Carlisle Gazette* printed handbills seeking the return of James Hamilton's peculiar Irish-accented mulatto slave. *Cumberland County Historical Society.*

to farming, and are allowed to be very skillful and active in that line. The Proprietor induced with a desire to decline farming, wishes to dispose of them, and will give one or two years credit, if required."

Clearly trying to appeal to both farmers and residents of urban York, the seller added as a postscript: "The Wench understands sewing, spinning and every kind of house work, as well as out work."[126] Not dissimilar was an advertisement from downtown York for a "likely Negroe Girl, [about] fifteen years of age, has had the Small Pox and Measles, and is duly registered." The seller explained to readers that there was "no other reason of disposing of her but the want of employment."[127] A Carlisle slaveholder sought to sell his bondsmen for a similar reason, citing a "want of having sufficient employment" for his "stout young Mulatto man." With no lack of racial overtones, he hoped a new master could "keep him from bad company—he would suit a farmer who would look after him."[128]

Although most slave sales were conducted on a buyer-seller basis, there are several recorded instances of auctions. In 1811, Jacob Upp of York advertised a "Negro wench…[w]ho has five years to serve, with a boy two years old. Also a mulatta girl, aged four years." He informed potential buyers that they would go "to the highest bidder" in an upcoming auction at his home.[129] Other slaves might find themselves sold at a public auction during estate sales.[130]

Chambersburg welcomed its own paper in the late 1790s, called the *Farmers' Register*. An October 1798 edition contained a brief article discussing the "Origin of the English dealing in African slaves." The editors alluded to the slave trade as a "barbarous traffic" that "has been the cause of so much misery in one part of the world." Try as they might, on the very same page a Peters township slave was offered for sale.[131] Another curious anecdote appeared in the *Farmers' Register* entitled "Effects of Slavery." It spoke of the writer's journey to a Caribbean plantation some eight years earlier, in which he observed a master "coldly order another of his negroes" to give one hundred lashes to another slave. "We were both of us struck with such astonishment, that, stupified [*sic*], pale, and shuddering, while the unhappy negro received the barbarous chastisement in silence, we looked at one another without being able to utter a single word." The writer went on to decry the master as "the dastardly perpetrator" of "the most atrocious injustice."[132] These columns apparently had little effect among local slaveholders, who neither manumitted their slaves nor ceased to advertise for runaways. Within a month, the *Farmers' Register* posted three slaves for sale from Mercersburg:

> FOR SALE,
> A Wench, who is a slave for life, and
> Two Boys, duly recorded, the oldest
> about six years, and the youngest near three

*years old, all healthy and smart. For terms apply
to the subscriber.   Patrick Campbell.
Mercersburg, June 20, 1798.*[133]

Other similar advertisements followed in the *Farmers' Register.* Walter McKinnie of Peters township placed a "likely, smart negro wench, about forty years of age" for sale in August 1798. "She is very active at both out and in doors work," he wrote, "and is regularly recorded."[134] In February 1799, another slot ran for the "time of a mulatto boy, brought up to country business, stout and active; he has a number of years to serve, and is recorded agreeably to law."[135]

With the gradual abolition law in place, many families lived each and every day on the excruciating divide between bondage and freedom. In November 1785, the *Carlisle Gazette* advertised an enslaved mother and her four children:

To Be Sold
A likely, healthy, negro wench, is used to do kitchen work, she has four children, the eldest a girl about 8 years of age; the second a boy about five years old; they are Registered, have had the small-pox and meazles [sic]*; the third a boy 3 years old; the youngest a girl about 18 months old; they are healthy and thriving, will be sold together for cash public securities at their current value, or bar-iron.
Enquire of the Printers.*[136]

The compromises of the gradual abolition bill left this mother faced with the heart-wrenching task of raising a splintered family. While her two youngest children could look forward to freedom on their twenty-eighth birthdays, her eldest daughter (and possibly her five-year-old son), who were but a few years older, would remain slaves for life, like herself.

Slave owners were not eager to discuss the eventualities of freedom for many slave children and seldom did so. The murkiness and lack of clarity surrounding the eventual freedom of two, possibly three, of this woman's children is not unusual. Some South Central Pennsylvania slaveholders would use both ignorance and technicalities to their advantage. With the dawning of the 1790s, many of the term slaves began having children themselves. If slaveholders were to go by the fine print of the gradual abolition law, any children of the term slaves were free at birth—only those born of a mother who was a slave for life could be held to serve for twenty-eight years. Yet this legal fine print meant little to slave owners and was largely unknown by those who would be wrongly enslaved.

One such case from Cumberland County went to the Supreme Court of Pennsylvania in 1823. A Carlisle slave named Nelly wanted to claim her freedom by citing errors found on her mother Rachel's registration document. Rachel was born in November 1780 and registered by John Duncan, a Carlisle merchant. Thus, Rachel was a term slave herself, and Nelly—the child she bore at age fifteen in 1795—was free at birth. Yet instead, Nelly was left completely in the dark about the freedom that was hers. She would not receive justice from the court, however, which overruled the claims of faulty registration and did nothing to free Nelly. It would take three more years for the court to affirm that only children of those who were slaves for life could be held until they were twenty-eight.[137]

Term slavery played an important role in court proceedings about Lett, a female term slave claimed by East Pennsborough farmer and millwright Thomas Fisher. The East Pennsborough slave owner reported that Lett ran away on October 25, 1806. She somehow managed to cross the Susquehanna and reach Harrisburg, where she was apprehended and sent to the Dauphin County jail within a few days. Fisher complained that he was "put to great expense and trouble" to regain Lett, and by "great expense and trouble" Fisher no doubt was referring to the forty-dollar reward he paid, more than three dollars in jail-related expenses, along with "two Dollars paid for printing handbills; besides the expense of advertising her in the Newspaper at Harrisburgh called the Guardian of Dauphin, [which was] two dollars…and also two dollars and an half paid…for advertising her in the Chambersburgh and Hagerstown papers." He even reported advertising in Bedford, Luzerne and Reading newspapers. After Lett had been captured, Thomas Fisher took the matter to court. There he asked county judges to extend Lett's term of slavery beyond twenty-eight years, to cover the damages he had incurred in searching for her.[138] Fisher's punctuality and hardline attitude were common among local slaveholders, who would use ingenuity to extend their use of slave labor as long as possible.

Chloe was born in East Pennsborough township in December 1782, the daughter of slaves owned by ferryman William Kelso.[139] Chloe's sad and troubled existence was yet another example of the intentional murkiness surrounding term slaves and their eventual freedom. She remained with the Kelso family until shortly after William's death, when in 1794 daughter Rebecca Kelso and her legal guardians arranged the sale of the "Negro Girl named Cloe" to Philadelphia merchant John Harland. Drawn up in haste and lacking attention to detail, Chloe's bill of sale and title transfer are riddled with errors, such as listing Chloe as "about sixteen years & five months" when in fact she was twelve. Yet, the document did acknowledge the term slavery nature of Chloe's situation—noting that her "Servitude will expire" on December 15, 1710—another blunder on this crude paper.

Harland had levied up 118 "Spanish milled Dollars" for Chloe in 1794, but by October of that year she had been sold once again, this time to another Philadelphian, Louis Martial Jacques Crousillat. Along with her, Chloe's new master received a growing package of documents, ranging from previous bills of sale to title transfers for Chloe. These documents would continue to be passed down through the line of Chloe's many owners. By March 1795, Crousillat sold Chloe to Oliver Pollock, who had been a commercial agent for the colonies in New Orleans, helping to finance the Revolution. In the early 1790s, Pollock returned to East Pennsborough, residing near his brother James, another slaveholder. Chloe thus traveled back across the state, to the very township where she had been born into term slavery some thirteen years before. With Pollock she remained for about a year and a half, when she was sold a final time for sixty-five pounds to Andrew Carothers, also of East Pennsborough.[140]

And so Chloe's time with the Carothers family began innocuously enough, amid the backdrop of hundreds of other slaves toiling in the vast countryside west of the Susquehanna. Through their young children, Andrew's wife, Mary, learned of some of Chloe's shortcomings, which she viewed as "laziness" that required discipline. Mary took the whip to the young woman on a relatively frequent basis, leaving Chloe convinced that her punishment was "far beyond the demerit of the fault." Mistreated and infuriated, Chloe embarked "to bring all the misery I possibly could upon the Family and particularly upon my Mistress."

She attempted to burn the barn but failed twice. Her thwarted attempts boiled up until late January, when Chloe drowned her masters' young daughter Lucetta. The discovery of their daughter's lifeless corpse shook the Carothers. As Andrew Carothers carried his daughter back toward the house, Mary rushed out of the home in horror. In a panicked frenzy, they rushed the young child inside and "tried all means to bring it to life," but to no avail. The other two children were quickly dispatched to alert the neighbors—and an impromptu wake was held in the midst of their neighbors, two other children and Chloe.

Mary Carothers later testified that there were "no odds in the negroes behavior that I took notice to in coming in and going out at the wake." Chloe believed "good days" were ahead of her "at least so long as my Mistress's trouble lasted," but it was not so. "The Funeral was scarcely over, being on Sunday, when she made me strip off my short gown, and gave me a severe whipping, with a cowskin; also on Tuesday she gave me another; and on the following Saturday she gave me a third." Chloe, now newly "determined upon further [r]evenge," repeated her act on their daughter Polly. What before had been a tragic accident soon turned to heightened suspicion, and Andrew Carothers whipped Chloe until he gained a confession—yet Chloe later revealed: "I was much more lashed by my own Conscience."

Chloe was taken to Carlisle, where she was put on trial, convicted and sentenced to hang for the murders of the two Carothers children—one aged four, the other six—in July 1801. The story quickly became sensational in the *Carlisle Gazette*, which considered the crime "perhaps unexampled in atrocity." After her death by noose, the *Gazette* ran Chloe's confession, which was taken by Reverend James Smith of Carlisle during her last days. Smith played up typical prevalent stereotypes, urging Chloe to admit that she "was much addicted to vice" specifically "vices, many of those of my colour are induced to commit," such as "profane Swearing."

Smith encouraged Chloe to look at her crimes as "temptations" and was remarkably fair in critiquing Mary Carothers for her whippings, although he remained steadfast that her misdoings did not justify Chloe's actions. There was also no mention that before committing the murders, Chloe was to be free at age twenty-eight. The Carothers, with frequent whippings, treated her as property, not as a servant who would one day become a free citizen. The *Gazette* also defined her as "Negro Chloe, the property of Mr. Andrew Carothers," a description devoid of any light of freedom. She was not educated and seldom was given any religious instruction—a fact to which Reverend Smith laid most of the blame for the crimes she committed.[141] Describing her life verbally, Chloe told Reverend Smith:

I was born a slave to Mr. William Kelso, who died when I was young, and willed me to his daughter Rebecca, in whose service I lived four years and an half, at the expiration of which time, I was sold to Mr. Oliver Pollock, with whom I lived about four years, who sold me to my late Master Mr. Andrew Carothers, with whom I lived, until I committed that greatest of crimes, for which, I am most justly condemn'd to die a shameful death. I never received an education; No pains were taken by any of my Owners, to instruct me in any duty I owed to God; Save while I lived with Mr. Pollock, I was taught my prayers, and other Duties, by his youngest daughter. But to my grief, I seldom said them; and when I did, it was in a very indifferent, and cold manner.[142]

Chloe was not the only slave in South Central Pennsylvania to face the noose. In 1788, a slave in northern Franklin County named Jack Durham was charged and convicted of rape. Jurors in the case included known slaveholders such as Henry Pawling, James Irwin, John McClellan and Robert Culbertson—at least four out of twelve jurors. That same jury considered Durham to be worth eighty dollars, which was paid as compensation to his owner, Andrew Long, by the state. Durham, on the other hand, was executed in July 1788.[143]

Many years removed from abolition, the lives of African Americans proved to be yet a terrible reality. Alongside the cases of Chloe and Jack Durham, the multitude of runaway slave ads prove that by and large, master-slave relations were animus, if not openly vicious. Not only was the slave's act of taking flight a clear indicator of their feelings, but the language used by masters seeking their return was very often bitter. Slave owner William Allison, for example, insinuated that his runaway might try and "steal" other clothing.

> *RANAWAY from the subscriber, in Franklin county, Pennsylvania, the night of the 14th instant, a Negro Man named TOM, five feet nine or ten inches high, twenty four years of age, stout made, had on a grey coating sailors jacket, the buttons the same of the cloth, three buttons on the sleeves, coarse shirting shirt, a pair striped ticking trowsers, old shoes, high crowned felt hat, it is likely he may steal other cloathing [sic], and will try to pass for a free negro. Whoever secures said fellow that I get him, shall have Ten Dollars Reward, and if brought home reasonable charges paid by WILLIAM ALLISON.*
> *October 16, 1793.*[144]

Allison was a farmer in Antrim township and had registered five slaves in 1780. Among those was a teenager named Tom, likely the same slave who thirteen years later finally opted to take flight.[145] Tom was recaptured at some point, and like many slave owners, a frustrated Allison decided to sell the young man. So in April 1794, he was sold to Thomas Cromwell, who lived well to the north at Bedford Furnace (in modern-day Huntingdon County). From there, Tom made another run for freedom by June—he was again described as "about 25 years of age, 5' 9" high, well made with a sour co[u]ntenance & a down look." Cromwell predicted that he "will most likely head towards Philadelphia or Baltimore."[146]

A few years later, Cumberland County slaveholder Hugh Smith of Hopewell township advertised a twelve-dollar reward for "a Negro woman aged about thirty years, had on a light Calico long gown, and short gown of the same, a red petticoat and a shawl, a new Roram hat, tied on with a black ribbon. Whoever secures the said negro woman in any goal [jail] so as the master may have her again, shall have the above reward and reasonable charges paid."[147]

Perhaps the most fascinating local runaway ad appeared in the *Carlisle Gazette* in June 1801. It was authored by John Williams of Allen township, who lived on the Yellow Breeches Creek, where he operated a farm with the labor of his slaves. In 1780, Williams had registered thirty-year-old female Sarah, eleven-year-old Nance and eleven-year-old Aleck as his slaves.[148] It was Aleck who seems to have captured Williams's attention the most with his intellectual prowess. However, after laboring to Williams's benefit for more than twenty years, Aleck, now a young man, decided to take flight:

> *TEN DOLLARS REWARD*
> *STOP THE RUN AWAY*
> *Ran away from the Subscriber, living on Yellow Breeches Creek, Cumberland county, Allen township, on Sunday the 14th of this instant, a Negro Man named Aleck—but no doubt will change his name. Had on when he went away a clouded jane coat, a spotted vest, corduroy over alls, new shoes, a wool hat almost new—can talk English and German, but English best—he is very fond of criticising in figures, or shewing his exploits in arithmetic—reads and writes English tolerable [tolerably] well, and can read German—about 28 or 29 years old, 5 feet 11 inches or 6 foot high, slim built, is very good at any farming business, and endeavours to excel in whatsoever he undertakes—has followed stilling. Whoever secures said Negro in any jail, so that the owner gets him again, shall have the above reward, and all reasonable charges paid if brought home, by JOHN WILLIAMS.[149]*

In neighboring East Pennsborough township, Alexander Parks ran away from his master a few years later:

THIRTY DOLLARS REWARD
RUNAWAY from the subscriber living in Cumberland county near to Carlisle, on Sunday the first of July, a mulatto man about 20 years of age, named ALEXANDER PARKS, about 5 feet, 5 inches high, well built, his hair black and curly, good features, speaks in a low hollow tone of voice, but can most certainly be known by a large mark of a cut on his right wrist near the thumb; he is active at farming business; had on and took with him a short blue coat, brown velvet jacket, one pair of tow trousers, an old muslin shirt, a good wool hat, and an old pair of shoes. Whoever takes up said servant, and secures him in any jail or otherwise so that his master can get him again, shall if taken near home, receive 4 dollars, if above ten miles, 6 dollars, if above 20 miles, 8 dollars, if above 40 miles, [illegible] dollars, if above 80 miles, 20 dollars if above 100 miles from home the above reward and all reasonable charges paid by
Joseph Junkin.
East Pennsborough township
July 7th, 1804.[150]

Thirty miles to the south, near Gettysburg, the sons of Colonel Robert McPherson were also slaveholders clinging onto the expiring institution. In 1805, his eldest son, William, a Revolutionary War veteran and legislator, offered a twenty-dollar reward for the return of "a Negro servant for years, named *Jim*, about 19 years of age, five feet eight inches high, slim made, remarkably knock kneed, especially the right knee, which stands very much in…took with him only his common wearing apparel consisting of a short coattee [*sic*] and overalls of home made cloth, winestone coloured, and jacket of the same, only striped in the weaving, and lighter coloured, a half-worn wool hat, gray yarn stockings, and shoes lately soled and parched."[151]

More than a decade later, William McPherson would advertise another runaway. This time, in 1818, he sought the return of a "Mulatto man named Jack Kelley, aged about fifty years, a slave for life—5 feet, 4 or 7 inches high; apt to get drunk, and when so, talkative…otherwise silent and inoffensive. Ad [*sic*] on a black cloth suit, and castor hat, other clothing not known. He ha[s] lost the bone of his right thumb, occasioned by a whitlow."[152] Another of Colonel McPherson's sons, Robert, also owned slaves. In 1810, he advertised for sale "[t]he time of an active, healthy *Young Negro Man*, who had about eight years to serve—is a good worker, and understands all kinds of farming business."[153]

Chapter Seven

"NO DOUBT SHE IS SOMEWHERE IN ADAMS COUNTY"

As slavery in South Central Pennsylvania began a slow, drawn-out erosion, questions about the righteousness of bondage reemerged under a different light. For years, fugitive slaves from neighboring Maryland and Virginia, and even the Carolinas, had been making their way north in search of freedom. The continuing flow of fugitives into the early nineteenth century forced residents to take sides. Before, Pennsylvania had been a slaveholding state—but now Pennsylvanians found themselves placed in the unique dilemma of reconsidering slavery as members of a free society. Would they, as citizens of a soon-to-be-free state, perhaps endlessly continue their part in maintaining "the peculiar institution" by helping to return the runaway "property" of their Southern neighbors? How would they treat a man or a woman's quest for freedom as residents of a state that had abolished slavery? These questions and more would mark the lines as the region took center stage in one of the most heated periods in American history.

For any fugitive making his or her way north, a great deal of intelligence and ingenuity was required, principally the ability to think on one's feet. Free or slave, a black person could be stopped by an inquisitive white citizen anywhere along the line—be it in Virginia, Maryland or Pennsylvania—and asked to produce a pass. If they themselves could not write, they would have to seek out someone they trusted who could and obtain a pass. The next priority for the runaway would be a change of apparel. Slaves were often poorly clad, and the hardscrabble clothing they wore was often distinctly striped.

Slaveholders throughout Virginia, Maryland and Pennsylvania were quite familiar with what it took for a successful escape. Almost routinely in their ads, slave owners caution readers that their fugitives may have obtained a pass somewhere—or, after providing a description of their apparel, adding that they were likely to change their clothes. An advertisement in Gettysburg's *Adams Centinel* speculated that Bob, a fugitive slave from Frederick County, Maryland, will "most likely…alter his name," also noting that "it is supposed he has procured a pass from some free Negro." Further, Bob's owner believed that "most likely he will change his dress."[154] Another Frederick County slaveholder expressed a similar thought, writing in his advertisement, "I think it highly probable he will change both name and clothing; possibly he may have a counterfeit pass."[155]

Taking flight, fugitives placed themselves up against herculean odds to successfully make their way to liberty. Many of the brief spurts of freedom enjoyed by runaways came to an abrupt end with the screeching sound of a closing jail door in Chambersburg, Gettysburg, York or Carlisle. Once jailed, much of the fugitive's fate rested on which county they were arrested in. During the 1780s, the York jailer evidently had a policy of selling African Americans if they were not claimed within four weeks—including those who claimed they were free.[156]

Those who found themselves in the Gettysburg jail in newly formed Adams County seem to have fared better. In May 1805, a man named Ned Butler was seized and brought to the Adams County jail on suspicion of being a runaway. "[H]e says that he is free, and lived in and about Greensburg. He is a stout fellow, five feet nine or ten inches high, says he is 23 years of age, a good countenance, stammers in his speech; he has with him a mixt broad cloth coat, with gilt yellow buttons, the name and likeness of *Thomas Jefferson* on each button." The Gettysburg jailer announced his intention to hold Butler until July 4, and if no owner appeared, "he will be discharged," rather than sold.[157]

A few years later, a runaway from Virginia named Ralph was brought to the Adams County jail, but when no one came to claim him, he was let free. However, his master took out advertisements, and Ralph soon found himself in another jail, only to scale the walls of the prison and continue his run. His master, in Virginia, believed it was "probable he will aim for Philadelphia or Baltimore." He warned readers that Ralph "is an artful cunning fellow, and I expect when accosted will show a discharge from the Prothonotary of Adams county for John Scott and Robert Wheeler, which last name he passed when first apprehended."[158] The residents of

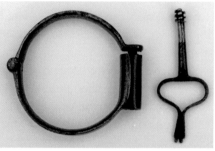

For centuries, slave owners employed a wide variety of iron collars to hinder their slaves' movements. Charles from Kentucky was spotted in Gettysburg with a neck collar; however, other fugitives might be identified by a locking collar on their ankles. *J. Howard Wert Gettysburg Collection.*

Handbills such as this 1832 imprint were a part of everyday life in South Central Pennsylvania. Geographic location drew runaways like Pris to the region. *Cumberland County Historical Society.*

Gettysburg had little doubt about the status of Charles, a fugitive spotted donning an iron collar around his neck. He hailed from Kentucky, "with an iron collar about his neck, says he is a slave the property of Mr. William Campbell, near Lexington, Kentucky, and that he ran away about the 1st of August last." This knowledge in hand, the jailer advertised his presence but retained his usual policy. "His master is desired to come and take him away, otherwise he will be discharged."[159]

Gettysburg in particular had become a hot spot for fugitive slaves fleeing anywhere from the Carolinas to Virginia to neighboring Maryland. "No doubt she is somewhere in Adams county, Pennsylvania, as she has been there before," cautioned a Maryland slave owner in 1821.[160] Slaveholders knew this and regularly advertised for runaways in Gettysburg's *Adams Centinel* as well as newspapers in York, Chambersburg, Carlisle and Harrisburg. The residents of South Central Pennsylvania, many of whom remained adamant slaveholders well into the nineteenth century, would be enticed with monetary rewards if they were simply to return runaway slaves to their local county jail—or an even larger sum if they were to return the slave to a location nearer the fugitive's master. Yet there were many families in the region who had not owned slaves, either by choice or for lack of economic means—how would they fall?

If residents were looking for guidance, the 1793 fugitive slave law passed by Congress would have encouraged them to see fugitive bondsmen and women as escaped property. The law clearly stated that even past state lines, a slave was a slave. The law also outlined a process by which slave owners or agents employed on their behalf were to go about reclaiming their property. They were to appear before a judge—be it a federal judge or city, county or town magistrate—where they had found the fugitive and declare the person whom they had caught as their property. This opened a loophole in which Pennsylvania's free black and newly freed slave population might fall into and be claimed as slaves and taken southward.[161]

This was the disconcerting reality that confronted the Pennsylvania Society for Promoting the Abolition of Slavery (Pennsylvania Abolition Society or PAS, for short). Based in Philadelphia, where it drew most of its membership, the Pennsylvania Abolition Society acted as a watchdog for slaveholders who disregarded state or federal laws. The rural countryside surrounding Gettysburg was laden with antislavery-minded individuals, and prior to 1820, Adams County produced more members of the Pennsylvania Abolition Society than Lancaster, York or Chester Counties.

Although the society dedicated its official purpose to be the promoting of new laws and enforcement of existing laws, those who were willing to lend their name and support to the society were often the same men who would help fugitive slaves on their way to freedom. The growing presence of thousands of free blacks in South Central Pennsylvania intermixed with these white abolitionists offered a formidable opponent to slave catchers seeking fugitives. In Adams County, the four members of the PAS were Jesse Russell, Nicholas Wireman, George Wilson and Samuel Wright—many of whom would be consistently involved in antislavery activities for decades to come.[162] Documentation is far weaker on the part played by free blacks, yet from what does survive, it is clear that white abolitionists and freed blacks worked in coordination and did so often. In 1794, former slave Samuel Mers sought to notify other African Americans when he advertised rather boldly in a York paper that he now resided there and could be "found by applying to Members of the Society for the Abolition of Slavery."[163]

Some of the very men who were no doubt assisting fugitives came forward quite publicly on October 28, 1820, at the Menallen Township Friends' Meetinghouse. There, a handful of local residents established "A *Society* to protect the sable descendants of Africa from being unlawfully held and dragged into bondage."

When, after a free communication of ideas on the subject, it was unanimously agreed, as the sentiment of all present, that SLAVERY is, in itself, inconsistent with the principles of Christianity; that it has a powerful influence in demoralizing the human family; and is an absolute violation of our bill of rights; that it is a stigma of the deepest die on the character of this boasted land of liberty, which time and perseverance in the cause of emancipation can only erase; and that it would be an act truly worthy of every real philanthropist, to use his influence to assist in eradicating its baneful [pres]ence from our borders.[164]

The society drafted its constitution and unanimously voted to bear the name "The Adams County Protection Society." They made clear that

[t]*he object of the Society is not to interfere between Masters and Slaves; but to use all proper means to prevent Kidnapping, and such coloured persons, as it may have ample ground to believe are by law entitled to freedom, from being violently seized and dragged into bondage by slave-holders and soul-drivers in the adjacent States; or as we have reason to believe has frequently been the case, under the shadow of law, partly for want of assistance in making a proper defence* [sic], *from being triumphantly borne off, probably to drag out a wretched existence of oppression and treatement, which humanity shrinks form the idea of delineating.*

This bold and revolutionary statement was signed and sent to the *Adams Centinel* for publication. The names of only two men appeared next to it, that of Jesse Russell, the group's elected president (and a member of the Pennsylvania Abolition Society), and Isaac Pearson, its secretary.[165] Both Russell's involvement and the group's stated purpose leave little doubt that the Adams County Protection Society was inspired by the PAS. However, nothing more was heard from the Adams County Protection Society, which vanished from the papers after its initial declaration.

The men who composed the short-lived Adams County Protection Society would have no doubt rejoiced at Pennsylvania's 1826 law that put in strict penalties for kidnapping free African Americans. Under this new law, a slave owner was required to appear before a local judge, where he would swear under oath that the individual was indeed his slave. The burden of proof also rested upon the slaveholder or his agent, and he was required to provide a legal affidavit from his home county or township as proof of ownership. This affidavit would include the slave's name, age and general

This image—a rallying cry of the abolitionist movement—was utilized by John Greenleaf Whittier for a poetic broadside. A poet and noted abolitionist, Whittier was known to visit Adams County on occasion. *Library of Congress.*

physical description, which a local judge would then review and compare to the alleged fugitive standing before him. Only if the judge was convinced that the fugitive described and the individual before him were one in the same would a warrant of removal be issued, which then allowed a slave owner to proceed home with his reclaimed property.[166]

Around the same time, to the north in Cumberland County, a vacuum left by the absence of outright abolitionist sentiment was filled with the "Cumberland County Colonization Society." The colonization craze began in the 1810s and ramped up with influential supporters throughout the following decades. Among the most prominent drum beaters for colonization was Kentucky senator Henry Clay, who helped to bring colonization prominence throughout the country with his ardent support. Colonization in a nutshell proposed to gradually free slaves and then recolonize them on the African continent.

Cumberland County's slaveholders and influential men read Clay's speeches—either when they consumed multiple columns of the local papers or in pamphlets that were printed and disbursed under the close watch of politicians to ensure their message got out. The Kentuckian believed that "no human law…could enforce a union between the two races." Yet he outright acknowledged slavery as a sin, adding that anyone who hoped for perpetual slavery "must go back to the era of our Liberty and independence, and muzzle the cannon which thunders its annual joyous return." For its introduction, he blamed the British government, noting it was under their "misrule this curse has been entailed upon us." However, he asked his followers to "show we are not willing accomplices in this crime of that government. If we do not, we may still continue to reproach that government; but we may be assured, that posterity will include us in the same reproach. There is also a higher tribunal, to which, unless we do every thing in our power to reduce the evil, we shall be made responsible for its continuance."[167]

This, and other encouragement, had prompted several prominent residents to form the Cumberland County Colonization Society, which was to be a branch of the nationwide American Colonization Society, with which Kentucky's Henry Clay was so closely affiliated. The Cumberland County organization declared its intents were "*First*, To provide for Colonizing and civilizing Africa through the direct instrumentality of Coloured Emigrants form the United States—*Second*, To promote, by all legal and constitutional means, the intellectual and moral improvement of the African race." The society requested an annual membership or "subscription" fee of twenty-five cents, $15 to be a member for life, or $100 to be a "director" for life within the organization. It also slated meetings to be twice a year, one on the first Monday in January and again on July 4.[168]

Yet neither Gettysburg, Carlisle nor the neighboring towns and countryside were free from slavery themselves. The vast majority of local slaveholders were doggedly determined to squeeze every year of service possible out of term slaves. In one issue alone of Gettysburg's *Adams Centinel*, both "a stout, healthy *Negro Man*, 24 years of age," with four years left to serve, and a second "stout, healthy Negro, who has 11 years left to serve," were advertised on the same front page.[169] Another ad in 1822 offered for sale "the time of a Negro Boy, [about] nine years old."[170] Nearly verbatim were two more postings, one in 1823 for "the time of a Negro Girl, [who] is 13 years of age, and has to serve until 28," and another in 1819 for "the time of a Mulatto Girl, who has near six years to serve," adding that "[s]he can be well recommended."[171]

Still, many term slaves felt compelled to escape. In 1822, York County slaveholder Peter Wolford sought the return of a term slave named Isaac. "[H]e may call himself *Cato*," Wolford warned. "He is 21 years of age and has 7 years to serve; he is about 6 feet high, stout made, middling dark color, tolerable[,] active, pleasant when spoken to, can play the Violin, and speaks the German and English languages." Isaac wore a "drab colored" coat, pantaloons, a striped jacket, a rorum hat and a pair of Jefferson boots. "He has perhaps fifteen or twenty Dollars…with him—and will probably, endeavor to pass for a Freeman."[172]

Everywhere else in Pennsylvania, slavery had fallen by the wayside. However, it remained alive and well in Cumberland, York, Franklin and Adams Counties, the distinctive geographic region bounded on the east by the Susquehanna River and on the west by the Blue Ridge Mountains. In 1790, the area was home to 28 percent of the slaves in Pennsylvania, and by 1810 its share had risen to more than 60 percent. Slavery took different courses in each of the counties, but York, Franklin and Adams had all seen a slow decline. By 1800, York County had just 77 slaves, while Adams County held 114. Within another decade, the numbers fell to just 22 and 71, respectively. Bondage in Franklin County had also been on the decline, from 330 slaves in 1790 to 181 in 1800. Come 1810, that number shrank to 87 slaves.

The first wave of term slaves born in 1780 would have become free in 1808, and every year following would mark the liberation of many more term slaves. That, along with the passing of an older generation of slaves, contributed to the slow decline of bondsmen. However, despite the trends of its neighbors, slavery in Cumberland County remained tenaciously stagnant, actually growing marginally from 223 slaves in 1790 to 228 in 1800. By the time 1810 rolled around, the number had jumped to 307 bondsmen out of 795 slaves statewide—meaning that nearly 40 percent of all the slaves in Pennsylvania labored in Cumberland County alone. As a whole, in 1810, the four counties accounted for nearly 500 slaves out of 795 statewide.[173]

Slavery's resilience in Cumberland County can be attributed to several factors, perhaps most significantly that of faith. Whereas parts of Adams

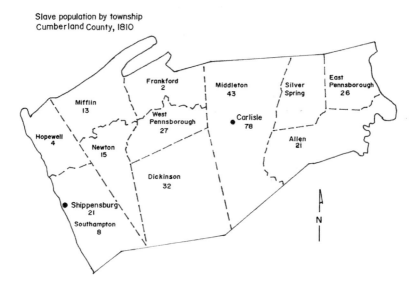

Slave population by township
Cumberland County, 1810

Slaves in Cumberland County, 1810. *Map by John Heiser.*

and York Counties had strong Quaker presence, Cumberland County was predominantly Presbyterian, and most Presbyterian slaveholders received little, if any, pressure to break connections with slavery.[174] The absence of religious pressure left most Cumberland County slaveholders to focus mostly on economic incentive. As a commodity of labor, slavery was a crucial moving force in society, and gradual abolition appears to have left most opinions on slavery unchanged in Cumberland County, even thirty years after its passage.

Yet in South Central Pennsylvania, slavery did not merely continue through passive actions on the part of slaveholders. Its continuation required slaveholders who were both active and single-minded in their resolve to protract an abolished institution for as long as they possibly could. These efforts varied from muddying interpretations of the law to scrupulously registering and using the labor of term-slave children. After the gradual abolition, Cumberland County recorded nearly 400 term slave births—including 298 slave children born from 1790 to 1826. The county saw as many as 18 slave births in one year (both in 1794 and 1795) and as few as 3, 4 or 5 births per year throughout the late 1810s.[175] Adams County, on the other hand, registered 109 term slave births between 1800 and 1820.[176]

Slaves continued to bring considerable prices. In 1809, a "certain Negro Girl named 'Esther' aged about six years" from Dauphin County sold

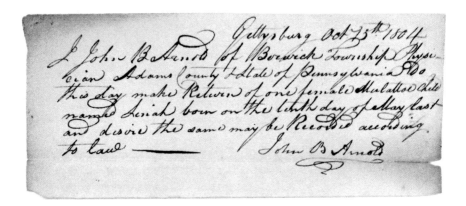

Above: In Adams County, Dr. John B. Arnold registered a mulatto girl named Sinah, born on May 10, 1804. *J. Howard Wert Gettysburg Collection.*

Left: A widow residing near Middlesex Mills in Cumberland County, Sarah Eliza Blaine registered no fewer than six slave births from 1807 to 1817. This 1816 registration denotes the birth of a girl "named Rachel daughter of My Mulattoe Wench Nelly." *Clerk of Courts, Cumberland County Archives.*

to Jacob M. Haldeman of Cumberland for $120.[177] A few years later, in October 1818, an estate inventory of Allen township slave owner William Bryson listed four term slaves: a "mulatto Boy to serve 18 years" valued at $200; two more mulatto boys, with 23 and 25 years left to serve, appraised respectively at $150 and $80. There was also a mulatto girl who had 20 years to serve, valued at $100.[178]

There are rare cases of slaveholders giving their bondsmen a distant glimmer of freedom; however, such acts were usually carried out through wills and would only take effect after a master had passed and could no longer use their labor. Matthew Loudon of East Pennsborough township wrote his will in 1799, bequeathing "the use or service of Black Sall until she is thirty years old." Back in 1780, Loudon had journeyed to Carlisle to register three slaves—a man named Dover, age twenty-four; a "Negro Wench" named Tyra, aged nineteen; and one child, nine-month-old Sall. If Sall was nine months old when he registered her in September 1780, that would mean she was born in January 1780—just weeks before the gradual abolition bill's mark of March 1, 1780. Yet Loudon nonetheless set her on similar terms—that she would be free at age thirty.[179]

Other sporadic acts of benevolence followed. In 1806, two slave owners permitted a wedding in Carlisle's First Presbyterian Church between their two slaves, Francis Lewis and Peggy Stansbury.[180] To the south, in Gettysburg, Lewis Johnston earned the unique title (alongside York's John Madison) of black slaveholder when he registered the birth of a male term slave named Stephen in March 1816. Johnston had married a black woman named Dolly Wilson in 1814; in all likelihood Dolly was a slave, and this was their son. If Johnston indeed was the husband and father of slaves whom he owned by law, it appears he later freed them to overcome this legal technicality by 1820.[181]

Chapter Eight

SONS OF THE REVOLUTION, FATHERS OF ABOLITION

In June 1835, a failed New York politician decided to leave behind his latest electoral defeat and head southward for the summer, with his family in tow. The caravan arrived in Harrisburg, where the family found quarters at a home within. "[T]he servants are all colored," he wrote, "and neat in their personal appearance. It is midsummer here, the honeysuckles, pinks, etc., are in full bloom, and there are ripe strawberries on the table."

Their spirits "rested and refreshed," on Monday morning the party crossed the Susquehanna and rode the fifteen-mile trek to Carlisle. "The country there is highly cultivated, and exhibits the appearance of much wealth and ease." This affluent and laid-back appearance was unique to this part of Pennsylvania, he noted, and "[a]s far north as Carlisle the places begin to assume the peculiar appearance which belongs to southern towns all over the world. The public square, carefully preserved shade-trees, balconies, and verandas, indicate to the traveler that he is arrived in a more genial clime." What he also noticed in this region of Pennsylvania—once again distinguishing it from other parts of the state—was its population. "The southern part of Pennsylvania discovers...a great augmentation of the negro population, with all its different shades of color. It is the emigration ground, or rather the city of refuge, of fugitive slaves, each of whom, once securely settled after the danger of pursuit is over, furnishes in his cabin a harboring-place for others who seek the same mode of emancipation."[182]

His name was William Henry Seward, and during the next thirty years he would develop some radical ideas about slavery—beliefs that led him to the forefront of the famous debates in Congress throughout the 1850s and nearly to the presidency. A one-time rival to Abraham Lincoln, Seward would become his secretary of state and a close confidant throughout the entire Civil War and the effort to abolish slavery. His future celebrity notwithstanding, Seward's observations offer an outsider's point of view into what was to be one of the most turbulent regions in America for the next three decades.

By the time of Seward's journey in June 1835, there were still a sprinkling of slaves remaining in South Central Pennsylvania. After 1810, the extent of bondage had diminished rapidly. Each year, a new group of term slaves turned twenty-eight and gained their freedom. A sporadic set of slave owners still clinging to their bondsmen remained around the time of Seward's visit—in

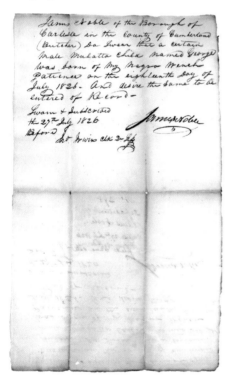

1840, some sixty years after gradual abolition, Adams County held two slaves; Cumberland, twenty-four; Franklin, none; and York, one.[183] The value of labor was not lost on these slaveholders or many in the general public, who still sought to extract profit during slavery's final days in Pennsylvania. In 1827, the *Adams Centinel* advertised for sale "the time of a stout Negro Girl, between 16 and 17 years of age, who has to serve until 28."[184] Even as late as 1829, Gettysburg's paper advertised "the time of a Negro Boy, Free at 28 years of age, who has two years and nine months to serve."[185]

The last registered slave birth in Cumberland County came in July 1826, when Carlisle butcher James Noble's slave Patience gave birth to a "mulatto child named George." Between 1811 and 1826, Noble registered seven slave births. *Clerk of Courts, Cumberland County Archives.*

Relief came for the few remaining slaves in 1847, when Pennsylvania abolished slavery outright.[186] However, abuses of the state's still-standing indentured servant laws ran rampant, and slaveholders in Maryland and Virginia seeking to relocate could simply free their slaves and then indenture them before bringing them into the commonwealth. In 1839, William D. Seymour of Virginia did just that, freeing his slave Jacob, under the agreement that Jacob would be indentured "to be a servant...in the State of Pennsylvania...for the full term of seven years."[187]

In the meantime, a growing community of antislavery activists were sowing seeds of their own discontent with the institution. With a unique fusion of Quaker presence and a bevy of interconnected, like-minded families, the Adams County countryside was home to some of the earliest antislavery activities recorded in South Central Pennsylvania. In 1820, Jesse Russell and a handful of others had formed the short-lived Adams County Protection Society, decrying bondage and offering itself to protect the rights of African Americans. A core group of Adams County citizens had long found slavery troubling. With the onset of the 1830s—and a new national dialogue concerning slavery—these same men who had met and discussed the topic for years among themselves decided the time was right to make a bold and very public statement.

In northern Adams County was a region outside the town of Petersburg (also called York Springs) known as Quaker Valley. The lush, fertile farming region was home to a number of Quaker families, including the Wrights,

A piece of abolitionist folk art from Quaker Valley entitled *Sheep Shearing and Anti-Slavery Discussion. J. Howard Wert Gettysburg Collection.*

Wiermans and Griests. These families not only lived in close proximity for decades, but many of their children had intermarried, forming strong bonds between them. Among those raised in Quaker Valley was William Wright. Growing up, both William's uncle and cousin were abolitionists. William soon had a farm of his own, three sons and three daughters by wife Phoebe, herself a Wierman daughter. In 1819, William had his first experience with a fugitive slave, one who his brother-in-law, Joel Wierman, had helped to elude slave catchers. The incident had a lasting impact, spurring William Wright into a lifelong activism to aid runaway bondsmen.[188]

In southern Adams County, immediately surrounding Gettysburg, were several networks of abolitionist families. Southeast of Gettysburg, leading into town along the Baltimore pike were the farms and abodes of William Young, Adam Wert and James McAllister, three leaders who helped to spearhead Adams County's antislavery movement.[189] A few miles up the Baltimore Pike, in the town of Gettysburg itself, were Robert W. Middleton and Thaddeus Stevens. Stevens, a Vermont native, had settled in Gettysburg in 1816, opening up a law office on the town square. As a young lawyer, Stevens appealed a case involving a slave mother and her two children attempting to free herself by claiming that she had been living in Pennsylvania for six months. Stevens, however, represented the slave owner, and he won the case with skill, returning the mother and her children to bondage. Although it remains unclear, the case may have been a turning point for Stevens and his views on slavery, if he had entertained any before, and he soon joined others in Gettysburg and the surrounding countryside as an antislavery activist. At the Fourth of July celebration in 1823, he was heard to toast: "The next President—May he be a freeman, who never riveted fetters on a human slave."

In 1833, the controversial lawyer was elected to represent Gettysburg in the state legislature, then meeting in Harrisburg. As might be expected of a politician, his support for the local antislavery movement was subtle and mostly behind the scenes, where Stevens's political string pulling shined. Throughout the 1820s and 1830s, while in Gettysburg, he exerted incredible influence as a trustee of the budding Pennsylvania College (later Gettysburg College) and perhaps most importantly as director and counsel for the Bank of Gettysburg. According to other abolitionists, Stevens would routinely threaten to apply financial pressure on debts to anyone who might speak out about fugitive slaves.[190] Middleton, a close ally of Stevens's, was the editor of Gettysburg's *Star and Republican Banner*, a paper that became the organ of local abolitionists.

Thaddeus Stevens represented Gettysburg in the state legislature before removing to Lancaster, which he later represented in Congress. *Library of Congress.*

It was no coincidence that this conglomerate of antislavery men decided to hold their largest gathering yet on the sixtieth anniversary of American independence, July 4, 1836. Many of them were the sons or grandsons of Revolutionary War soldiers, and it was to the Declaration of Independence that these men looked when they decried slavery. In their eyes, the existence of the "peculiar institution" defied the spirit of "all men are created equal."

Thus, on Monday, July 4, 1836, "a number of the *freemen* of Adams county" gathered at James McAllister's mill, located directly off the Baltimore pike on Rock Creek. The meeting's host, James McAllister, was called to the chair, while his neighbors, William Young and Adam Wert, were appointed secretaries. The group proceeded to read and "unanimously adopt" fourteen resolutions. They began with the statement "[t]hat we receive as a Divine truth the declaration made by St. Paul at Athens…that 'God hath made of *one blood* all nations of men.'" This was followed by a flurry of references to the Declaration of Independence and the American Revolution, references that were not tossed around lightly by these sons and grandsons of Revolutionary veterans.

2. Resolved, That we recognize the truth in the declaration made by the American Congress at Philadelphia in the year 1776, that "ALL MEN ARE CREATED EQUAL."

3. Resolved, That we concur with the Signers of the Declaration of American Independence in declaring, that "ALL MEN are endowed by their Creator with certain unalienable rights, among which are life, liberty, and the pursuit of happiness."

4. Resolved, That, if liberty is the right of all men, no human being can be rightfully held in slavery.

5. Resolved, That we cannot agree with those who profess to be opposed to slavery in the abstract, and who at the same time can find many excuses for slavery in practice; because, in our view, the whole evil of slavery consists in the practice of it, the discontinuance of which would be a complete removal of the evil.

6. Resolved, "That with a firm reliance on the protection of Divine Providence," we will make a diligent use of all proper means to procure the abolition of slavery.[191]

Eight more resolutions followed, varying from expressing their belief that Congress should abolish slavery in the District of Columbia; a blunt threat to vote only for congressional candidates who supported abolition; and finally encouraging freedom of speech. Drawing on the very enlightenment ideas for which their fathers and grandfathers had fought for, their eleventh resolution read:

11. Resolved, That the freemen of the United States ought never to permit their minds to be fettered, their lips to be sealed, or their presses to be muzzled on any subject, because the progressive improvement of the human race requires, that every subject, having any relation to man, should be constantly open for examination, and that every individual should be fully at liberty to "prove all things" by the light of revelation, the light of reason, and the other accumulating light of experience.[192]

Their fourteenth and final resolution acknowledged the backlash they would soon receive but reassured readers that they were doubly determined to make their voices heard:

14. Resolved, That although we may be denounced, for our efforts in the cause of human rights, by office-holding and office seeking politicians, and even by men wearing clerical robes, we will not be "afraid of their terror," but, disregarding their denunciations, we will continue to open our mouths for the dumb, and to plead the cause of the oppressed and of those who have none to help them, humbly believing, that, if we do unto others as we wish that they would do unto us, we shall have the approbation of Him who will render to every man, according to his works, and whose approbation will be a full remuneration for the loss of this world's favor.[193]

All fourteen of the meeting's resolutions were run in Robert Middleton's *Gettysburg Republican Star and Banner*, under the headline *"Freedom vs. Slavery."* Middleton, himself among the interconnected web of Adams County abolitionists, published a friendly introduction to the resolutions. He referred to them as "the proceedings of a number of intelligent gentlemen celebrating the 4th of July at McAllister's Mill." He then continued under his own pen, stressing "the Liberty of Speech and the right of Free Discussion" and denouncing Northern support of slavery as "trembling subservience…to the haughty bearing of Southern task-masters."[194]

Several months later, on Constitution Day, September 17, 1836, many of the same men assembled once again several miles down the Baltimore Pike at the modest settlement of Two Taverns. The Two Taverns meeting was a noteworthy change from "the program of the past," because it was publicly advertised in advance and open to anyone. At this meeting, Robert Young was appointed president, Andrew Little and Cornelius Houghtelin as vice-presidents and Josiah Benner the secretary. The meeting was largely composed of friends and neighbors—the man who stood up and offered another series of fourteen resolutions was Adam Wert, who lived next to Houghtelin and near Young and McAllister.

Many of the resolutions emphasized the importance of freedom of speech—another invoked the "Golden Rule," declaring, "The holding or selling of human beings, as property, *is not* doing unto others as we wish that they should do unto us; and, therefore, the institution of Slavery is a direct and constant violation of that grand rule of human conduct." They even quoted slaveholder Thomas Jefferson, reminding listeners and readers of the *Star and Banner* what the third president had once written: "I tremble for my country when I reflect that God is just and that His justice cannot sleep forever."

The concluding resolutions turned focus on a more material goal—the abolition of slavery in the District of Columbia. "We are desirous to be represented in the next Congress by a man who will embrace the earliest and every opportunity to vote for the abolition of Slavery and the Slave-trade in the said District," read the twelfth resolution, "and who will not be deterred from the discharge of duty by threats of dissolution of the Union, nor by threats of any other kind whatsoever." The meeting concluded with the understanding that several of the men would form a committee "for the purpose of procuring the appointment of a time and place for the holding of [an] *Anti-Slavery County Meeting*."[195]

The first meeting of the newly borne Adams County Anti-Slavery Society was to be held in the county courthouse on December 3, 1836. In the early afternoon, the leaders of the local antislavery movement were greeted by a fully packed courthouse, with no standing room. Yet this crowd was in fact a product of several proslavery thinkers, who feared the loss of Southern business if their town were to be turned into an antislavery mouthpiece. Realizing the trap had been sprung, the men who had attended the meeting at McAllister's on July 4, and at Two Taverns on September 17, attempted to abandon the courthouse and a sure doom to this hostile audience. "Hoots, jeers, cat-calls, oaths, and whistles arose from the swaying crowd, as the little band of the faithful tried to force their way through the mass towards the doors." Eggs were thrown, "and the odor that arose therefrom was abominable." One "practical wag" among the riotous audience hurled a dead cat into the mix of the chaos.

Undeterred, the antislavery men made their way from the courthouse and into the nearby Gettysburg Academy, where they determined to have an evening meeting.[196] They set about drafting a constitution, based on seven principles:

1. *That God has made of one blood all nations of men.*
2. *That all men are created equal.*
3. *That all men are endowed by their Creator with a right to liberty, and that this right is inalienable.*
4. *That no human being can be rightfully held in slavery.*
5. *That the holding or selling of any human being as property, is a sin against God, and a crime against man.*
6. *That immediate emancipation is the right of every slave, and the duty of every slaveholder.*
7. *That obedience to the divine commands us at all times, and under all circumstances, consistent with perfect safety.*

The constitution that was drafted that evening, in the spirit of these seven principles, outlined the practical means through which these abolitionists hoped to change public sentiment. They would be called "The Adams County Anti-Slavery Society," and their three enumerated objects were first, the "entire abolition of slavery in the United States"; second, the "intellectual and moral improvement of the colored population"; and finally, the "destruction of those prejudices which are found on a mere difference of complexion, without regard to character."

Membership of the society was open to any person who was a not a slave owner, at a membership fee of one dollar. The society would have a president, two vice-presidents, a secretary and a treasurer, who would all be elected annually on the first Saturday of December. Ever aware that their mission required convincing the broader electorate, they also made sure to include a clause that public notice "shall be given in one or more of the public papers of every meeting of the Society." The document was signed by more than twenty men, among whom were James McAllister, Jesse Russell, William Wright, Adam Wert, Jacob Wierman, Josiah Benner, William Reynolds, Jacob Griest, Robert W. Middleton, Isaac Tudor and others. For many of these men, attending this inaugural meeting required a lengthy trip from the countryside into town—William Wright and Jacob Griest had made the lengthy journey to Gettysburg from their homes in Quaker Valley, situated more than ten miles to the north.

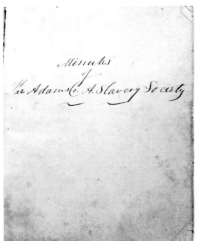

Not surprisingly, the society chose to hold its next meeting in Quaker Valley, a friendlier locale where many of its dedicated members resided. The society met on a Saturday afternoon in January 1837 at the Petersburg Academy, in York Springs. "Several thrilling and pertinent addresses were…delivered upon the relation which Pennsylvania & the North generally bear to Slavery, & the propriety & constitutionality of our course defended."

This otherwise ordinary composition book was used to record the minutes of the Adams County Anti-Slavery Society. *J. Howard Wert Gettysburg Collection.*

Many of the abolitionists were also intertwined with the temperance movement, and at their behest, a resolution was passed "that the members of this society earnestly & affectionately entreat the colored people of Adams Co. to abstain entirely from the use of any kind of drink containing alcohol." Bearing in mind the age-old stereotypes against free blacks, they no doubt feared what the sight of one intoxicated freeman might do to the credibility of their entire movement. The care and finesse which their movement required reveals the enormity of the task they were undertaking.

The society continued meeting over the following years, both in Gettysburg and the York Springs area. They tackled a wide variety of tasks, from appointing delegates to represent Adams County in antislavery conventions, to attempts at public outreach, petitions to Congress and even group-led protests. "Whereas, the most odious system of human oppression—American Slavery—derives its most efficient support from the purchase of the produce of Slave-labor by those who are not Slave-holders," the group resolved in December 1837 that "the members of this Society will not purchase any article of Merchandize which shall have been produced by the labor of American Slaves."

Among the group's members, there was no lack of fervency. When the society failed to meet on the Fourth of July in 1837, a concerned Joel Wierman sought to convene the group as soon as possible. "I deeply regret that the fourth of last month passed by without our holding a meeting," he penned to Adam Wert. "I think the times call for an increase of energetic action." Wierman, a Quaker, appropriately signed his letter: "In hast[e] I am thine in the cause of the oppressed."

Working closely with the Adams County Anti-Slavery Society were multiple women, appointed by the Philadelphia Female Anti-Slavery Society "to circulate petitions in Adams Co. in order to procure signers thereto." These women, as recorded in an 1837 communique, included Mrs. J. Barnity in New Oxford, Mary Grier in Gettysburg, Mrs. D. Withers in Fairfield and Lydia Wierman in York Springs. "It is requested," their Philadelphia contact added, "that no female under the age of sixteen should sign the petitions."

Laden with countryside intellectuals, the group began allotting funds to accumulate a small, communal library ripe with antislavery literature. In 1838, they subscribed for six issues of the *Pennsylvania Freeman*, an abolitionist paper published in Philadelphia. Once received, the papers were to be distributed among members "for the use of this society." They also began to accumulate a small array of books, such as William Jay's 1839 *A View of the Action of the Federal Government, in behalf of Slavery*, which survives with a marking on the inset, "York Springs A.S. Society No. 4," a name garnered by the group's frequent meetings there.

The trek to York Springs, however, was a time-consuming endeavor for those living near Gettysburg, and attendance among members from southern Adams County dipped. After a poorly attended January 1839 meeting, Allen Robinette penned Adam Wert "to inform you that we were much disappointed at, not finding any of our Gettysburg & Mount Joy friends present at our last meeting, our friends from Menallen were all present, & in this Neighborhood none were absent." Writing from his classroom, Robinette—a school teacher from Latimore township—provided Wert with a brief summary of the last meeting and the date of the next, adding that "your attendance at the next, & indeed all Meetings would be very desirable if at all convenient to yourself, but if not will you be so good as to Correspond with us & aid us by your Counsell." Asking Wert's opinion on an upcoming state senate election, Robinette apologized for his "incoherent" dispatch, "as I am engaged in teaching school, & my attention is almost entirely engaged with the noise around me."

Plagued by a dispersed membership with travel woes, the society lost steam as it entered the 1840s and by 1850 was no longer a cohesive or publicly advertised group.[197] However, during its existence, the Adams County Anti-Slavery Society had given a collective voice to its diverse fellowship of rural farmers and town-bound professors and editors. No comparable group in the region had spoken so poignantly or so consistently against slavery. The end of the society did not change the hearts and minds of those who had so earnestly joined it—they remained staunchly devoted to the cause and would soon discover their finest hour outside the watchful eye of the law.

Chapter Nine

"COME IN AND TAKE THY BREAKFAST"

The Underground Railroad in South Central Pennsylvania

Hope, fear, dread, terror, love, sorrow, and deep melancholy were mingled in my mind together; my mental state was one of the most painful distraction. When I looked at my numerous family—a beloved father and mother, eleven brothers and sisters...but when I looked at slavery...in its mildest form, with all its annoyances; and above all, when I remembered that one of the chief annoyances of slavery, in the most mild form, is the liability of being at any moment sold into the worst form; it seemed that no consideration, not even that of life itself, could tempt me to give up the thought of flight.

So wrote twenty-year-old James Pembroke, who had been born into slavery on a plantation along the Maryland's Eastern Shore. These thoughts came to mind on a Sunday, a day of worship, which, in Maryland, slaves were usually given a respite from work—although this was often scrapped during peak harvest seasons. "Most of the slaves were resting about their quarters," he recalled, "others had leave to visit their friends on other plantations, and were absent." As he walked about the plantation on this quiet, calm mid-November day, the young man's mind was cluttered. Pembroke had already taken steps to prepare for a run northward—he had hidden a bundle of nondescript clothing amid some rocks a short distance away.

"It is impossible for me now to recollect all the perplexing thoughts that passed through my mind during that forenoon; it was a day of heartaching to me." He grappled with the question of telling his family and loved ones about his decision to flee—would they be suspected as silent helpers—would they, he wondered anxiously, "be sold off as a disaffected family." Nor did he know exactly what lay ahead. "I have no knowledge of distance or direction. I know that Pennsylvania is a free state, but I know not where its soil begins, or where that of Maryland ends?" On top of that, it was common understanding that "there was no safety in Pennsylvania…for a fugitive, except in lurking-places, or under the care of judicious friends, who could be entrusted not only with liberty, but also with life itself."

As the clock struck 2:00 p.m., Pembroke realized "the hour was come, and the man must act, or for ever be a slave." He entered the home and grabbed the "only morsel I could see in the shape of food," a piece of bread, which he secreted in his pocket. Taking a last glance at his unhappy home, he "sallied forth thoughtfully and melancholy, and after crossing the barn-yard, a few moments' walk brought me to a small cave." There, in a pile of rocks, he had hidden his bundle of clothes. He changed and then proceeded north "through thick and heavy woods and back lands."

Years before, when Pembroke was eight or nine, he and his elder brother Robert had been sent to Hagerstown to apprentice with tradesmen in the town. Sending out slave children was a common practice among slaveholders, who could forgo the costs of having to feed and clothe a child during the years he would be less productive on the plantation. In the meantime, the bondsman would gain valuable trade experience, which would benefit his master in the future. Pembroke spent two years in the home of a Hagerstown stone mason as an apprentice. "When I returned home at the age of eleven," he remembered, "I was set about assisting to do the mason-work of a new smith's shop." Over the course of nine years of ensuing work, James would garner a reputation as a "first-rate blacksmith."

This all flashed before Pembroke's mind as he approached Hagerstown on that placid Sunday afternoon in November 1828. He was grappling with whether or not to pay a visit to his brother Robert, who had remained in Hagerstown, and inform him of his intentions. However, to do so would put not only himself at risk but also his brother. On top of that, he also understood the necessity of passing through Hagerstown at night. "I was well-known there, and…any intelligence of my having been seen there would at once put the pursuers on my track."

Sullenly and quietly, James toiled through Hagerstown without arousing any notice. "I now found myself under cover of the night, a solitary wanderer from home and friends; my only course was the north star, by this I knew my general course northward, but at what point I should strike Penn[sylvania], or when and where I should find a friend, I knew not." He determined to make his flight "rapid" and set about a relentless trek to cover as much ground before the revealing glare of dawn.

He continued as such until around 3:00 a.m., when "the chilling effects of the dew" set in. "At this moment, gloom and melancholy again spread through my whole soul. The prospect of utter destitution which threatened me was more than I could bear, and my heart began to melt. What substance is there in a piece of dry Indian bread; what nourishment is there in it to warm the nerves of one already chilled to the heart?" Immersed in gloom, dawn snuck up on Pembroke, who hastily made use of a corn shock, "the only shelter I could find...in the midst of an open extent of country." The shock was located but a "few hundred yards from the road," and Pembroke was forced to remain in a squatting position the entire day. By nightfall, he had devoured his rations—the single loaf of bread. "[N]ot a crumb of my crust remained, and I was hungry and began to feel the desperation of distress."

It was at this point when many fugitives seeking freedom began to falter. "As I travelled I felt my strength failing and my spirits wavered; my mind was in a deep and melancholy dream. It was cloudy; I could not see my star, and had serious misgivings about my course." Doubts began to seep in as endurance was tested. A journey through a countryside filled with slave catchers and reward seekers was a dangerous task even for a well-fed and well-nourished person. The twenty-year-old managed to trudge on through the night, and at dawn he discovered a few "sour apples," before secreting himself underneath the arch of a bridge, where he spent his second day in hiding.

"I felt quite satisfied that I could not pass another twenty-four hours without nourishment," he later recalled. "I made but little progress during the night, and often sat down, and slept frequently fifteen or twenty minutes." At dawn on the third day, exasperated as he was, James threw caution to the wind and meandered to a public turnpike. There a young boy operating the tollgate informed the fugitive that he was eighteen miles from Baltimore—Pembroke, who knew his master lived eighty miles from the city, was astounded that he had trekked sixty-two miles. "That distance in the right direction," he lamented, "would have placed me several miles across Mason and Dixon's line, but I was evidently yet in the state of Maryland."

Later that morning, James encountered "a young man with a load of hay." Drawing up his horses, the man spoke "in a very kind tone," inquiring where he was headed, and if he was free. When asked if he had "free papers" on him, Pembroke replied that he did not. "Well, my friend, you should not travel on this road: you will be taken up before you have gone three miles. There are men living on this road who are constantly on the look-out for your people; and it is seldom that one escapes them who attempts to pass by day." The man then pointed out the way for James to get off the road, and gave him directions to find "a certain house, where I would meet with an old gentleman who would…advise me."

So taken aback was Pembroke that "in ten minutes I had so far forgotten his directions as to deem it unwise to attempt to follow them, lest I should miss my way and get into evil hands." He eventually returned to the road, and just like the young man had warned him, he encountered a man who hollered out to him, "Who do *you* belong to?" James replied that he was free, and after admitting he had no papers on him, refused to stop for the man, who shouted threats and soon came walking after him.

"I saw that a crisis was at hand; I had no weapons of any kind, not even a pocket-knife; but I asked myself, shall I surrender without a struggle. The instinctive answer was 'No.'" James decided that he would continue to walk, run if necessary, and was confident that "my habits as a blacksmith had given my eye and hand such mechanical skill, that I felt quite sure that if I could only get a stone in my hand, and have time to wield it, I should not miss." The pursuer was evidently no athlete, and Pembroke must have breathed a momentary sigh of relief when he heard the man begin to huff and puff and fall behind. Yet the man quickly yelled out to another, a shoemaker armed with a knife, who ran out and grasped the twenty-year-old fugitive by the collar while the other wrestled control of his arms. Two more men, evidently their friends, stood by watching, creating a seemingly hopeless fate for Pembroke. "My heart melted away, I sunk…into the hands of my captors, who dragged me immediately into the tavern which was near."

A crowd of gawkers and onlookers gathered around the tavern to see the runaway, who still insisted he was free. His captors dragged him back and forth to the homes of two magistrates—neither of whom were at home. As the afternoon wore on, his captors became somewhat lax, and as they struggled getting Pembroke, with his hands bound and tied, over the multitude of fences dotting the countryside, they untied him. When the group neared the tavern, James made another break into a small belt of woods. "One of my captors was walking on either side of me," he recalled, "I made a sudden turn, with my left arm sweeping the legs of one of my captors from under him…and took to my heels. As soon as they could recover they both took after me."

For someone in James Pembroke's shoes, the most trivial of things might make the difference between a lifetime spent in slavery or a new life in freedom. As fate would have it, James's running start and his ability to quickly scale a fence gave him a sufficient head start to make a dash for the woods. As he crested the hill, suddenly a man ploughing the intervening field seized him by the collar, and he was a captive once again. As they trudged back to the tavern, James received kicks, punches and profanity from the infuriated men. However, Pembroke conceived a ruse for his next escape attempt. He came "clean" and informed them that "a few weeks ago, I was sold from the eastern shore to a slave-trader, who had a large gang, and set out for Georgia, but when he got to a town in Virginia, he was taken sick, and died with the small-pox…No one claimed us, or wished to have anything to do with us; I left the rest, and thought I would go somewhere and get work."

All lies, of course, excepting that Pembroke was from a plantation on the Eastern Shore. He could perceive several reactions in his favor immediately—it seemed to be believed by those present, including his captors, despite the tensions and escape attempt, he perceived "a murmur of approbation." He also noticed "that a panic began to seize some, at the idea that I was one of a small-pox gang. Several who had clustered near me, moved off to a respectful distance." His ruse worked, and the men decided not to imprison him but rather sought to employ him for the time being. One of the local magistrates who had been absent earlier in the day spoke of his intention to hire him for twenty-five cents a day. After "cheerfully" agreeing to the magistrate's offer, Pembroke was told he would spend the night at the tavern with his captor.

James still felt very uneasy among these men, so when his captor was moving a team of horses into the barn for the night, he made yet another break, this time successfully. After a long trek that night, Pembroke found a barn and crawled in the corn bed, where he managed to arouse the ire of the family dog. "I had at once great fears that this mischievous little thing would betray me," he wrote. He remained in the corn crib all day long, with intermittent but unsuccessful barking by the dog. Toward evening, he heard a party on horseback pass by and listened with terror as they trotted toward the house. He recognized the voice of his former captor, who bellowed out to a laborer on the farm asking if he had seen a runaway. Most chillingly, Pembroke learned that his ruse from the day before would no longer work with his old captors should he once again fall into their hands. He listened intently as the man explained, "A party of us have been after him all day; we have been up to the line, but can't hear or see anything of him. I heard this morning where he came from. He is a blacksmith, and a stiff reward is out for him, two hundred dollars."

The laborer's reply, "He is worth looking for," could not have soothed James's worries either. At night, much to his relief, he left the barn and continued on, at first through marshes and thickets until he eventually decided to return to the road. "All I could do was to keep my legs in motion, and this I continued to do with the utmost difficulty." He continued for several days, taking cover in corn fields and occasionally braving the roads during daylight, when on Saturday morning he came upon a tollgate "attended by an elderly woman." James asked her if he was in Pennsylvania, to which she replied he was—much to his good fortune, Pembroke had trekked through fields and roads to the east of Gettysburg and now found himself at a small town in northern Adams County known as Petersburg, or York Springs. Deducing his situation, the woman advised him to go to the home of William Wright, "a Quaker who lived about three miles from her, whom I would find to take an interest in me."

From the area of York Springs, Pembroke made his way through meandering hills and a winding roadbed to the home of William Wright, comfortably situated at the base of one of the many rolling hills in the mountainous locale. Wright would behold quite the sight when he opened his door and saw a "trembling" James Pembroke on his stoop. Behind Wright and the open door, James eyed a "comfortably spread table," laden with a delectable country breakfast. As instructed, he told Wright that he had been sent in search of employment. "Well," the Quaker responded, "Come in and take thy breakfast, and get warm, and we will talk about it; thee must be cold without any coat."

Those words spoken by a stranger, but with such an air of simple sincerity and fatherly kindness, made an overwhelming impression upon my mind. They made me feel, spite of all my fear and timidity, that I had, in the providence of God, found a friend and a home. He at once gained my confidence; and I felt that I might confide to him a fact which I had, as yet, confided to no one.

From that day to this, whenever I discover the least disposition in my heart to disregard the wretched condition of any poor or distressed persons with whom I meet, I call to mind these words—"Come in and take thy breakfast, and get warm." They invariably remind me of what I was at that time; my condition was as wretched as that of any human being can possibly be, with the exception of the loss of health or reason. I had but four pieces of clothing about my person…I was a starving fugitive, without home or friends—a reward offered for my person in the public papers—pursued by cruel manhunters…Had he turned me away, I must have perished. Nay, he took me in, and gave me of his food, and shared with me his own garments. Such treatment I had never before received at the hands of any white man.[198]

Quaker Valley runs through an idyllic strip of northern Adams County, amid apple orchards, winding roads and ever-undulating hills, curving near the base of the South Mountain range. The sporadic settlement of farms in this region left much land yet un-cleared, and the thickly wooded slopes of the various hills and ridges offered bountiful cover to any fugitive on the run. It was here that a handful of Quaker families had settled in the 1730s and remained for generations as a tightly knit religious and community group.

Born in December 1788, William Wright was nearing forty when the fugitive blacksmith appeared on his porch. A well-rounded scholar, as a young man William had worked as a schoolteacher, but health difficulties had removed him from the classroom. In 1820, he and wife Phebe resided along the road leading north from Gettysburg to Carlisle in a home called Woodburn. The house was situated among a mountainous backdrop (near the base of the small town of Idaville) and only a few miles due west from York Springs. The Wrights could take some comfort in the fact that they were surrounded by fellow Quakers, among whom were Phebe's brother, Joel Wierman, who was also known to help fugitives. Even in their least active state, neighboring Quakers were still "passive helpers" to the Wrights and were highly unlikely to report another Friend who was following their religious doctrine by aiding a fugitive.[199] A short distance

Quaker William Wright of Adams County was one of the most fervent abolitionists in the country and guided hundreds of fugitives to freedom. *From* Pennsylvania at the Jamestown Exposition, *1908.*

to the southwest was a budding African American community on Pine Hill, later known as Yellow Hill.[200]

James would spend six months with the Wrights, a stint of hospitality that would change his life forever. Wright quickly offered Pembroke employment in sawing and splitting cords of wood for the coming winter, for which he offered the fugitive "liberal pay and board." "The idea of beginning to earn something," the former slave wrote, "was very pleasant." Wright, who already had experience in helping fugitives, explained "the way and means of avoiding surprise" in the event any slave catchers should come in search of the blacksmith.[201]

Wright, a former teacher, soon turned his attention to James's education. Pembroke explained that he could not read or write: "My duties as a blacksmith have made me acquainted with the figures on the common mechanics' square. There was a day-book kept in the shop, in which the overseer usually charged the smithwork we did for the neighbours. I have spent entire Sabbaths looking over the pages of that book; knowing the names of persons to whom certain pieces of work were charged, together with their prices, I strove anxiously to learn to write in this way." Intrigued, Wright handed him a slate and pencil, adding: "Let me see how thee makes letters; try such as thou has been able to make easily." James proceeded to make out a spattering of letters—A, B, C, L and G. Phebe Wright, standing close by, observed the fugitive's penmanship with wonderment, remarking: "Why, those are better than I can make." "Oh, we can soon get thee in the way, James," William assured him.

"Arithmetic and astronomy became my favourite studies," James later wrote. William Wright was a well versed country intellectual, whose presence exerted a great influence on the twenty-one-year-old. "He is one of the most far-sighted and practical men I ever met with," recalled the fugitive. "He taught me by familiar conversations, illustrating his themes by diagrams on the slate, so that I caught his ideas with ease and rapidity."

"I now began to see, for the first time, the extent of mischief slavery had done to me. Twenty-one years of my life were gone, never again to return, and I was as profoundly ignorant, comparatively, as a child five years old... As my friend poured light into my mind, I saw the darkness; it amazed and grieved me beyond description." When he became discouraged under the weight of the educational disadvantage he faced, Wright was quick to dazzle James with stories of African American intellectuals whom he had never before known of, such as poets Phillis Wheatley of Boston, Francis Williams of Jamaica and almanac maker Benjamin Banneker.

"How often have I regretted that the six months I spent in the family of" William Wright, wrote James, "could not have been six years. The danger of recapture, however, rendered it utterly imprudent that I should remain longer." Leaving in early March 1829, Pembroke "wended my way in deep sorrow and melancholy, onward towards Philadelphia," where he would stay with another Quaker farmer.[202]

William Wright would continue to open his home as a place of refuge for countless fugitive slaves during the ensuing decades. He also found a lifelong friend in James William Charles Pennington, whose new name contained a tribute to the Quaker—he added the "William" for William Wright. "I have been twice to see him within four years," Pennington wrote in 1849, "and have regular correspondence with him." So prized was Pennington's friendship that the Wright children eagerly desired to be the first to open his letters when they arrived. James, now fully literate, had since made history when he became Yale's first black student and went on to a career as a popular orator, abolitionist and minister in New York. "Thy name is mentioned almost everyday," Phebe assured him. In his 1849 autobiography, *The Fugitive Blacksmith*, Pennington spoke of William and Phebe Wright only as "W.W" and "P.W." to conceal their identities because they were still active agents in the Underground Railroad. So much so that the preface of Pennington's book contains an excerpted letter from William, reading: "We have a man here from the eastern shore of thy state [Maryland]. He is trying to learn as fast as thee did when here."[203]

The experiences of James W.C. Pennington offer not only a glimpse into the extraordinary generosity and bravery of William and Phebe Wright but also the journeys of countless thousands of fugitives who sought sanctuary from bondage. The Underground Railroad in South Central Pennsylvania was not a clearly delineated, stop-by-stop circuit. Rather, it was a spattering of homes in the rural countryside and in towns both large and small. The men and women, both white and black, who would act as "conductors" on the Underground Railroad were usually "cocooned" in, with devoted friends or family nearby who would either actively help or look the other way when need be. Yet for most runaways, such as Pennington, their ability to find these homes—or friendly people to direct them there—was largely based on luck. If he had not escaped his captors' clutches in northern Maryland, James Pennington would have easily been whisked back to his former master the following day.

The "routes" of the Underground Railroad should not be viewed as clearly marked movements from one point to another but covert, often nighttime movements from one cluster of friendly homes to another. Any wrong step, however, could catapult a runaway back into bondage. There were many men—so-called slave catchers—who made their livings off of capturing and returning runaway slaves for their rewards, or sometimes selling other blacks into slavery and netting the profit. There were rarely any clear sanctuaries for the fugitive, and even some African American families throughout the region reportedly worked with slave catchers to get a piece of bounties on fugitives.[204]

Like Sam Davis of Virginia, most runaways set out perfectly oblivious to the existence of friendly locales. "I travelled on three days and nights, suffering for want of food," Davis later recalled. In Franklin County, he entered a shop to purchase food, eyeing with apprehension two musket-bearing men who came in behind him. "They had followed me from a village I had passed through a little before. They took me, and were going to carry me before a magistrate" in Chambersburg. "By and by, watching my chance, I jumped a fence and ran. They were on horseback. I got into a piece of woods, thence into a wheat field where I lay all day; from 9, A.M. until dark. I could not sleep for fear. At night I travelled on, walking until day, when I came to a colored man's house among [the] mountains. He gave me a good breakfast, for which I thank[ed] him, and then directed me on the route. I succeeded, after a while, in finding the underground railroad."[205]

This branding iron served as the inspiration for John Greenleaf Whittier's poem "The Branded Hand." A variety of branding irons similar to this were routinely employed by auctioneers and slave catchers in Hagerstown, Maryland, a central exchange area for slave trafficking. *J. Howard Wert Gettysburg Collection.*

Fugitives might expect to blend in and receive help among the large communities of free blacks near Mercersburg, Chambersburg, Gettysburg, Columbia, York, Carlisle and a spattering of other countryside settlements. A prominent Franklin County route ran through an African American

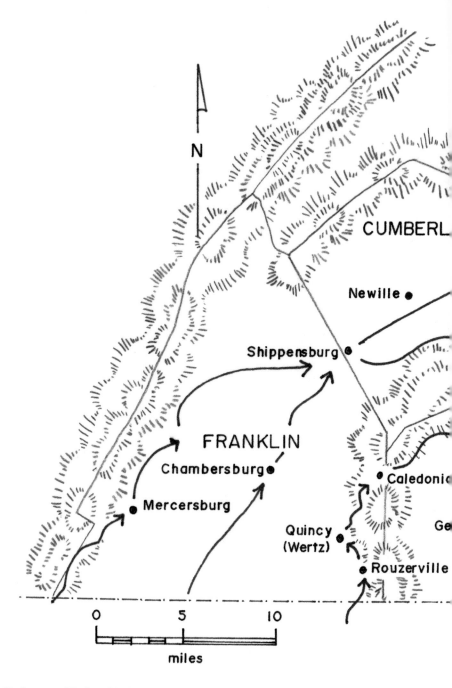

The Underground Railroad in South Central Pennsylvania. *Map by John Heiser.*

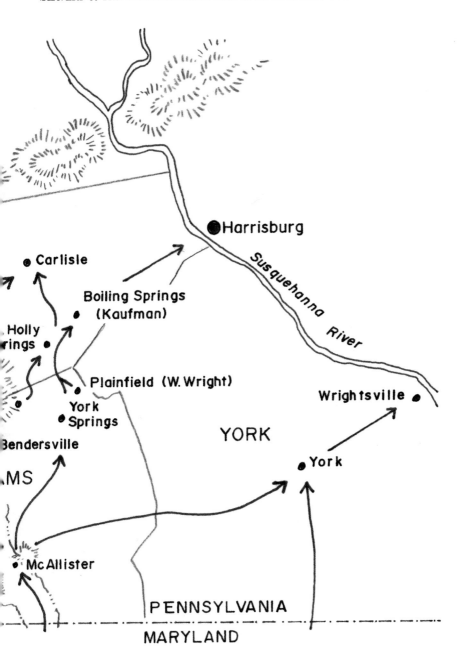

settlement about two miles west of Mercersburg, near the mountains, known as Little Africa (not to be confused with another "Little Africa" near Caledonia Furnace). The community was a turbulent location closely watched by slave catchers, and in 1837, several runaways chose to fight rather than be recaptured, killing a magistrate and wounding two slave catchers. Others traveling up the valley found themselves in Greencastle, where Moses Anderson sheltered runaways. "Among the earliest impressions made upon our childish mind were the tales of horror about the South told by the fleeing fugitive as he lay in the secret enclosure of my father's house where he was concealed," recalled Anderson's son, Matthew. From Greencastle or elsewhere, many runaways reached

Harriet Beecher Stowe's *Uncle Tom's Cabin* was a rallying cry for abolitionists in South Central Pennsylvania and throughout the country. This porcelain figure, portraying the character "Uncle Tom," belonged to an abolitionist family in Adams County. *J. Howard Wert Gettysburg Collection.*

Chambersburg, where they sought help from black residents there and then continued northward, while still others were under the care of Hiram Wertz.

Wertz's interest in the antislavery movement began when he was a young boy. He lived in Quincy, a small town on the western side of South Mountain in eastern Franklin County. In 1837, Matthew Dobbin of Gettysburg journeyed to his home, where he applied with Hiram's father for a position as a schoolteacher. He succeeded and, until his death in 1855, would board in the Wertz home. Dobbin was a native of Gettysburg, and it was his father, Reverend Alexander Dobbin, who in 1776 built the famous Dobbin house in southern Gettysburg, no doubt with the assistance of his two slaves. Alexander Dobbin bequeathed his widow "the remaining part of the time of my negro servant Lett" as he neared his death in 1808.

Matthew Dobbin, however, wanted nothing of the sort. As a young boy in the 1830s and 1840s, Wertz watched with intense interest as the elder teacher received a weekly newspaper from Washington entitled the *National Era*—a rabidly antislavery publication, which first published

Harriet Beecher Stowe's *Uncle Tom's Cabin* in serial form. "We all read the story as well as the sequel to it, which was published soon afterward in the same paper," recalled Wertz, "and this was one of the means that led me to become an anti-slavery boy."

Around 1845, as young Hiram grew closer to Matthew Dobbin, the latter soon confided in him that for "several years" he had been escorting fugitive slaves in their flights north. Noting that he was "getting old and feeble, he wanted me to succeed him in his mission of mercy," remembered Wertz. He recalled the route he inherited with vivid detail—fugitives who entered the state near Rouzerville, at the western base of South Mountain, were guided about eight miles north, using the mountain as a clear indicator of direction, to Hiram's father's barn in Quincy, "where they arrived generally in the very early morning and I fed them and guarded them during the day." Of the fugitives, he recalled, "Some were very…startled by every noise. Some were depressed and fearful that after all their efforts for freedom they might be caught and taken back to their old masters. Others were full of confidence and in high good humor over having crossed the Mason and Dixon line."

"When night came I led them north," he recalled, "about eight miles, to a settlement called Africa." Indeed, near Thaddeus Steven's Caledonia Furnace and the small village of Greenwood lay another village known as "Little Africa," where twenty to twenty-five African American families lived. In Greenwood lived Robert Black, "another Captain of the Underground Railroad," according to Wertz. "He saw to it that the fugitives were cared for, working along with William Hammett, then superintendent of Stephen's furnace, which was located two miles to the [e]ast of Greenwood. It would have been a sorrowful time," he opined, "for any one to have ventured into this neighborhood with the idea of attempting to arrest any fugitives."[206]

On the eastern side of the South Mountain, in Adams County, slaves were directed up the eastern slopes of the mountain to Quaker settlements near Bendersville, in northern Adams County, and from there to Carlisle or Harrisburg. These routes were primarily tapped by slaves coming from the Shenandoah Valley of Virginia or western Maryland. Fugitives fleeing from northeastern Virginia; the Washington, D.C. area; and eastern Maryland (like Pennington, from the Eastern Shore), would usually arrive in the vicinity of Gettysburg. For decades, the town of Gettysburg had been heavily patrolled by slave catchers, but a strong, close-knit African American community in the southwestern end of town provided aid to runaways. "Jack" Hopkins, the janitor of Pennsylvania College, and resident Mag Palm were among those purported to assist fugitives. Basil

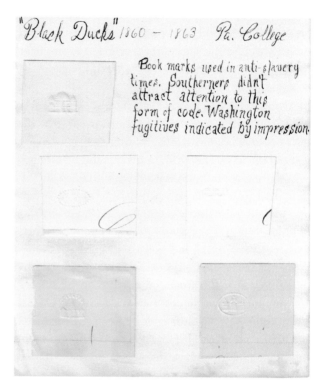

Right: Several Pennsylvania (later Gettysburg) College students who belonged to the "Black Ducks" fraternity took an active role in the Underground Railroad. College student J. Howard Wert, the son of abolitionist Adam Wert, preserved these notes with varying impressions that were used to communicate the location of fugitives to one another. *J. Howard Wert Gettysburg Collection.*

Below: A scene of rural life amid the network of abolitionists located southeast of Gettysburg. *J. Howard Wert Gettysburg Collection.*

Biggs, an African American farmer west of town, concealed runaways during the day and at night led them north to Edward Mathews, a free black living on "Yellow Hill" in Quaker Valley, some ten miles north of town. Others charted a course away from the dangers of Gettysburg and kept to the east, sometimes inadvertently, like Pennington.[207]

On the Baltimore Pike southeast of Gettysburg was another close-knit community of abolitionists. Farmers William Young, Adam Wert and Cornelius Houghtelin were ready to lend a hand; Adam Wert's young son later remembered a frantic carriage ride with a fugitive mulatto boy a short distance up the pike to James McAllister's mill, as slave catchers trailed several hundred yards behind in pursuit. McAllister had not only hosted the July 4, 1836 antislavery meeting at his mill but had also long been a friend of the fugitive. Of Scottish descent, the whole McAllister family were devoted antislavery activists—each and every one of his five stout sons would eventually enlist with vigor and passion in the Union army.

His mill was located along Rock Creek but a comfortable distance off the Baltimore Pike. Nearby, runaway slaves often hid in a cave on densely wooded Wolf Hill. The runaway mulatto whom Adam Wert and his son had directed to McAllister's mill was concealed by James Alexander McAllister (known as "Alleck"), one of the McAllister boys. He "had the mulatto securely ensconced in a snug rock cave." The young boy spent two nights at McAllister's, partly because slave catchers were in hot pursuit, and was then forwarded north to the Quaker stations in York Springs and eventually to Harrisburg. Often James McAllister would take upon himself the daring task of personally leading slaves northward—one of his sons, S.R. McAllister, later remembered that "[m]y Father staid [sic] at his [William Wright's] house several nights after transacting business with the Route."

The McAllisters also concealed fugitives in the cog-pit of the mill. The room had a thick, heavy door that had to be opened by a pulley above them and was further hidden from sight by the mill's massive water wheel. McAllister guided slaves either to the north, toward William Wright and others operating in Quaker Valley, or to the east, through York and then Columbia, Lancaster and on to Philadelphia.[208] Theodore McAllister, another of his sons, later recalled:

From 1850 to 1858 was the period in which they [fugitives] *came most frequently. I was during this time from eight to sixteen years of age. And many of these fugitives were neither seen nor heard of by any other member of our large family, except myself until they were far on their way to*

111

Canada. But there were never any questions asked, if quantities of rations disappeared from the cellar and pantry. And I notice old clothing was placed very conveniently to my hand on the garret of the old home. Crouched under the lower floor and in the cog-pit of that old mill, I listened to some horrible tales of cruelty told by those young, mostly yellow men, some of them with the features of the white race, as they rested their weary legs and filled themselves up in preparation for another race for the bleak north. Most of them ended their tale of woe in the same way, "I will never go back alive to see mothers, wives, sisters torn from their families, lashed together, and driven off, like cattle, to some far Southern slave mart."[209]

McAllister's reference to "mostly yellow men" refers to the complexion of the fugitives—meaning that most of the runaways through their Rock Creek station were mulattoes, bearing varying degrees of racial intermixture. One such fugitive came before the McAllisters in the form of an attractive young mulatto woman named Louisa. She was the slave of Georgia senator Robert Toombs and, allegedly, his mulatto daughter. S.R. McAllister later recalled that "his daughter was beautiful of light cream color about five feet six inches tall, splendid form, about twenty-two or three years old; would pass in Canada for a white lady." With the help of abolitionist Dr. William Chaplin, she and other slaves fled Washington in 1850. However, Chaplin's plan was sniffed out, and he and the fugitives aboard his wagon were confronted and ultimately recaptured.

Somehow, Louisa still managed an escape—either then or shortly thereafter—a fact corroborated by Toombs's own pen. "Nothing yet of Louisa," he wrote in late August. "I think it not unprobable that Louisa has gotten off to the North, poor fool!" A frustrated Toombs grumbled about the costs of "catching & trying…Chaplin the negro thief," which "will cost me a pretty round sum, I see the abolitionists of NYork are determined to rain thirty thousand dollars to defend him. To

Georgia senator Robert Toombs, who later served as the secretary of state for the Confederacy, was infuriated by his slave's escape via the Underground Railroad in Gettysburg. *Library of Congress.*

save counsel fees I think I shall appear against Chaplin myself & try & see whether thirty thousand dollars will save him from my clutches."[210]

Still others were guided eastward from the Gettysburg area to York, where a variety of men of interesting backgrounds were ready to assist them. Joel Fisher, Samuel Willis and William C. Goodridge were among the agents aiding fugitive slaves in York. Goodridge had been born a slave in Baltimore and at age six was dispatched to York so he could apprentice to a tanner. At age sixteen, he ran away from his apprenticeship and went to New York, where he learned to become a barber, only to return to York in 1840. Goodridge became an affluent businessman, selling toys, candies and even owning a line of railroad cars. He made use of his town house at 123 Philadelphia Street to secret fugitives and often relied on a black teamster named Cato Jourdon, who stowed fugitives in his wagon as he crossed the Wrightsville Bridge into Columbia.[211]

For those who were guided northward through Franklin or Adams Counties, there were several friendly regions in Cumberland County. Many slaves from Chambersburg journeyed northward toward Shippensburg. They might follow the Great Valley Turnpike, the railroad, obscure Indian trails that connected the two towns or simply the contours of the valley. In Shippensburg, Dr. Alexander Stewart was a reliable friend to the fugitive. Nearby, in the small village of Leesburg, wagon maker Samuel Taylor was known to trade blows with slave catchers. The Carlisle area was the next logical stop for any fugitives in Shippensburg, as well those in Adams County. Many of the slaves that Hiram Wertz had delivered to Caledonia traveled along the mountains to Mount Holly, where they might either split off north to Carlisle or northeast to Boiling Springs.

In Carlisle, there were a handful of devoted abolitionists ready to help fugitive slaves. John Peck was an African American barber who also worked as the Carlisle agent for the antislavery newspaper *Emancipator*.[212] Perhaps the most famous abolitionist in Carlisle was Dr. John McClintock. A professor at Dickinson College, McClintock rose to fame in June 1847 when a group of slaves had been claimed by two men from Hagerstown. As the slaves were about to be placed in the custody of the Marylanders, McClintock arrived at the courthouse to contest the proceedings, believing that the matter had not been conducted according to a new state law.

In the meantime, much of the free black community in Carlisle had come to the courthouse, and when the fugitives were brought out to be placed in a carriage, they rushed forward and overpowered "the slave-owners and constables...and a frightful melee ensued in the street, in which for some

This circa-1910 photograph depicts a "Crumbling station of [the] historic 'Underground Railroad' system" in Cumberland County, although the location is not specified. *Cumberland County Historical Society.*

minutes paving stones were hurled in showers and clubs and canes used with terrible energy." Two of the fugitives escaped, while another remained in custody. One of the slaveholders, James Kennedy, was "severely hurt, having been felled to the earth under a succession of blows from stones and clubs which completely disabled him," and later died from the violence. In the controversial trial that followed, McClintock, after being dragged through the mud and accused of inciting a riot, was acquitted, while thirteen others were convicted. Shockingly, eleven were sentenced to three years of solitary confinement at the Eastern Penitentiary. This unorthodox sentence from a controversial judge was later overturned.[213]

Whether coming north from Mount Holly or east from Shippensburg, fugitive slaves would encounter a cluster of safe houses in South Middletown township. Stephen Weakley's house was located a few miles south of Carlisle, near the Yellow Breeches Creek. From Weakley's, runaways would be shuffled into Boiling Springs, where Mode Griffith, Philip Brechbill, George Sailor and Daniel Kaufman would assist them. None played as significant and as dangerous a role as Kaufman, who had begun secreting slaves at age seventeen in what became known as Island Grove, a heavily wooded oasis on the Yellow Breeches, near Boiling Springs. Much like the Wrights and Wiermans to his south, Kaufman surrounded himself with a closely knit unit of like-minded individuals he could trust, such as his brother-in-law Stephen Weakley.

Most of the slaves Kaufman received in Boiling Springs had likely passed through Hiram Wertz's route along the South Mountain and through Little Africa, although many others came up the valley, through Chambersburg and Shippensburg, and from there east to Boiling Springs.[214] An example of the interaction between this close-knit group of abolitionists came one morning when Mode Griffith stumbled upon "9 grown negro men on the Ridge near Boiling Springs on their way to liberty" in broad daylight. Sensing the impending danger the fugitives were in, he rushed to inform Daniel Kaufman, and "through their joint efforts they were hidden in the dense thickets of Island Grove." Kaufman, however, had business in Carlisle, and on his way into town he encountered three men who were hunting for the runaways. With extreme caution, he returned to Boiling Springs and brought the fugitives into his home, one at a time, to eat late that evening. After they were all fed, he led the group toward Carlisle, where agents in the town guided them toward Harrisburg.

Another incident involved a family of slaves who, when advertised for sale in Hagerstown, fled and made their way through Chambersburg and Shippensburg, traveling east through Cumberland County on the Walnut Bottom road in broad daylight. Miraculously, they continued unmolested, at one point "feasting" on apples and cider and openly inquiring for directions to Daniel Kaufman's—they had evidently heard of his generosity somewhere along the way. When they reached Kaufman's around nightfall, he was alarmed to hear both that they had traveled in broad daylight and secondly that they had inquired at random of his whereabouts. Surely someone had spotted them—and word of where they were headed would soon reach slave catchers.

He loaded his wagon with straw, into which the family of fugitives was concealed, and he started out at midnight, backtracking toward Shippensburg to throw off any pursuers. The next night, friends in Shippensburg brought the family through Carlisle and across the Camelback bridge to Harrisburg. Crossing the famous toll bridge across the Susquehanna was done with relative ease by most abolitionists, as the tollkeepers were generally "in sympathy with the business," and once in Harrisburg the large free black community provided added security.[215]

Kaufman, however, would be forced from his Underground Railroad activities in the late 1840s, during one particularly heated legal case. The story begins with the 1846 death of an Arkansas slaveholder, who owned thirteen slaves. His widow, her four daughters and thirteen slaves came to live with a cousin in Williamsport, Maryland. Fearing they would be sold off and separated, the thirteen slaves ran away. They reached Chambersburg, where they garnered the assistance of free black George Cole, who led them through Shippensburg and all the way to Daniel Kaufman's barn, where he departed them. Sometime during the night, the fugitives disappeared in Kaufman's wagon.

It did not take long for John Stake, a cousin of the widow slave owner, to track the path of the fugitives to Daniel Kaufman's front door. What followed was a highly publicized trial, and in 1847, a Cumberland County court fined Daniel Kaufman $2,000 for aiding the runaways. However, this was soon overturned by Pennsylvania's Supreme Court, because Kaufman was errantly tried for a federal crime in a county court. The slaveholding family renewed their lawsuit in 1849, where in federal court the result was a hung jury. Kaufman's luck, however, ran out in 1852, when a second trial found him guilty and fined him $2,800 in damages and much more in other fees.

The case had attracted significant attention, especially among abolitionist groups, and Kaufman received support and counsel from the likes of Thaddeus Stevens. Faced with the swift hand of the law, Stephen Weakley stepped in and footed much of the $4,191 bill. He managed to raise $1,900 from abolitionists and sympathizers in Philadelphia, but the remaining $2,291 was "paid out of my own pocket." As Weakley explained, "I yielded up the money on the same principle I would to a highwayman. The costs were heavier than was anticipated, and a portion of them were thought to be illegal, but I had no remedy."[216]

After Kaufman's legal woes, John Morrison and Richard Woods would receive most of the fugitive traffic. Morrison and Woods lived adjacent to each other in Lower Dickinson township, southwest of Carlisle. The Yellow Breeches Creek ran through their properties, creating a "bit of swamp land" where they secreted fugitives. In addition to his Underground Railroad activities, Woods employed a number of free blacks who "walked down every day from the mountains" to work on his farm for eight dollars a month, the same wage he gave to any white workers.

It was Mike Buck, "a squat figured" black man, who led fugitives to Woods and Morrison. "He had gold earrings, and his head was always bound with a bandanna handkerchief," Woods's granddaughter later recalled. "In fact he resembled the pictures of pirates in the magazines today. No one knew from

A wagon laden with wooden rails is pictured at "Sandy Mount," the home of Jabez Gardner in Caroll County, Maryland. The Baltimore Pike passed through Carroll County on its way to Gettysburg, making the region a heavy traffic area for both commerce and fugitive slaves. *J. Howard Wert Gettysburg Collection.*

where he came, but he always said he had never been a slave. He lived in the mountains in a cabin provided by grandfather, Uncle John Sterrett." Buck would lead fugitives more than twenty miles from Caledonia, north along the mountains to Woods's home southwest of Carlisle. Stephen Weakley continued to lend a hand, and along with John Harder in Carlisle, they were able to forward fugitives safely to Harrisburg.[217]

For decades, numerous Northern states had passed personal liberty laws, which were used to make life difficult for slave catchers. However, these protective laws were cast aside when, as part of the Compromise of 1850, the Fugitive Slave Act was passed, amending and strengthening the 1793 law. The 1850 law made it "the duty" of both public servants to return fugitives to their masters or master's agents and forbade fugitives from testifying in their own trials. Yet for the men and women who composed the

This 1850 engraving, entitled "Effects of the Fugitive-Slave-Law," echoes the widespread frustrations felt by abolitionists across the country. In the scene, several men are ambushed by a group of slave catchers, who open fire from the adjoining cornfield. *Library of Congress.*

abolitionist community of South Central Pennsylvania, the biggest blow was found in Section 7, which threatened legal action against "any person who shall knowingly and willingly obstruct, hinder, or prevent" the recapture of a runaway or "harbor and conceal" a fugitive. Any violators would be liable to a $1,000 fine and six months in prison.[218]

Predictably, the Fugitive Slave Act was a great burden to the men and women who were already risking their lives and fortunes to help bondsmen and women to freedom. S.R. McAllister believed the law to be "the most infernal diabolical law ever…passed…It made stars and stripes a libel—and every man a Negro catcher." Helping fugitives, he noted, "got to be very risky as there was money in it and imprisonment back of it."[219]

Undeterred, William and Phebe Wright continued to risk their lives and fortunes helping fugitives. In 1840, the couple had moved several miles east, to a new home near York Springs. Already twenty-year veterans of the Underground Railroad, the Wrights seemed to have tailored the design of their new brick house, christened "Plainfield," for that exact purpose. Plainfield featured an unprecedented tally of doors, including a back door and outdoor staircase leading from the second story of the home, for quick exits. Below sat unusually wide basement windows, large enough for a human to enter or exit if need be.

Slave catchers were not oblivious to the Wrights' craft; however, Plainfield's location made it all but impossible to surprise the Quaker family. Anyone approaching on public roads could only reach Plainfield by passing either the Griest farm to the south or continuing north to an intersection of several roads, where the Deardorff farm sat. Either route, a slave catcher would be hard pressed to escape notice. Jacob Griest, who had been a member of the Adams County Anti-Slavery Society alongside William Wright, could easily sound the alarm, as could the Deardorffs, who it appears at the very least were passive helpers. Plainfield itself was set back from the nearest road in a slight depression, and the long, winding farm lane leading to the home provided the Wrights with even more time to conceal runaways.

Even these precautions could not protect fugitives who were working outdoors in full sight. In 1851, four barely clad slaves from Maryland made their way to William Wright's front porch. Learning that their pursuers were already ahead of them in Harrisburg, the Wrights thought it best to split the party up, sending two to brother-in-law Joel Wierman's nearby home, while the other two men remained with the Wrights. However, while working outdoors, the pursuers eyed the men, and in fright, they gave themselves up. William, well versed in deceiving slave catchers, directed the two men—Tom and Fenton—to go into the house and grab their coats. Meanwhile, he introduced the slaveholders to his wife. Grasping the look in her husband's eye, Phebe began to quiz the men: "Do you recognize the Scripture as the guide of your lives?" "Certainly, madame," replied one, "I am an elder in the Baptist church." Phebe swiftly procured a bible, and set about lecturing him on the sins of slaveholding. By the end of their forty-five-minute conversation, "his teeth chattered with terror."

Only then did the pursuers began to realize the ruse they had been dealt, and they demanded to see their slaves immediately. Wright replied that it was "not my business at all," slyly telling the gentlemen that it had been their obligation to take custody of Tom and Fenton when they had first seen them. Infuriated, they accused the Quaker of hiding their slaves, to which Wright again replied: "Haven't I been here all the time? How can I have concealed your slaves? If you have your lawful authority here is the house; search it. I shall not help you, but I can't prevent you." Tom, one of the runaways, had hid himself in the carriage house. The other, Fenton—the mulatto son of the Baptist elder—had concealed himself in a rye field. The slaveholders searched Wright's property, to no

The wife of William Wright, pious Quaker Phebe Wright established herself as one of the most dedicated figures in Adams County's Underground Railroad network. *From* Pennsylvania at the Jamestown Exposition, *1908.*

avail, and angrily departed, hoodwinked and enraged. "Now, gentlemen," Wright implored, "you will acknowledge that you have searched my house and outbuildings to your heart's content."

Another time, a large group of runaways arrived at the Wright home, including a mother with an infant child. Their masters were hot on their trail, and the Wrights had comfortably hidden all the fugitives, except the crying infant, who it seemed could not be silenced. A young woman who was staying with the Wrights at the time grabbed the child, caressing it like a mother in bed. As the slave catchers rudely searched the house, they opened the bedroom door to find the young white "mother" holding a baby draped in swaddling clothes. She gently pinched the baby to produce a cry, giving the full illusion to the slave catchers, who left empty handed. "I am glad they did not see the baby," Phebe later remarked.[220]

With newly emboldened slave catchers, life in South Central Pennsylvania became all the more hazardous for free African Americans. A mulatto man named John Butler, his wife and young daughter had settled in Cumberland County in 1858. The Butlers were a quiet, peaceable family, noted by their white neighbors "for sobriety, industry and general good conduct." They lived in Dickinson township, close to Stephen Weakley, Richard Woods and John Morrison. As comfortably as they were situated, one Friday night in June 1859, the Butlers were kidnapped. Their neighbors awoke the following morning to find the Butler cabin empty and eyed "articles of clothing strewn about, the half rumpled bed of the little girl, and bread left to rise on the hearth." "The secrecy with which the affair was conducted," opined the *Carlisle American*, "leaves little room to doubt but that the parties were well acquainted with both the neighborhood and their nefarious business."

To the Butlers' good fortune, the scattering of abolitionists who lived nearby would not simply forget them—John Morrison traveled along with Sheriff Robert McCartney to the Maryland border, where they captured two men involved in the kidnapping. Through their efforts, Butler and his family were later returned to Cumberland County.[221] Few, however, met with the same fortune as the Butlers did—countless fugitives and free blacks alike were overtaken by omnipresent slave catchers, never to be seen again.

Amid the presence of slave catchers and frightened fugitives, the region was graced by the presence of several nationally known abolitionists, including Frederick Douglass, William Lloyd Garrison, Benjamin Lundy, Jonathan Blanchard and even John Brown. As he plotted his slave uprising at Harpers Ferry, Brown initially made his headquarters in a Chambersburg home, under the comfort of an alias. Henry Watson, a black barber in Chambersburg,

John Brown's October 1859 raid on Harpers Ferry—and ensuing hanging—made him one of the most polarizing figures in the nation. Brown spent much of the prelude to his raid in Chambersburg under an alias. *Library of Congress.*

helped to arrange a meeting between Brown and Douglass, where the former's plans for a militant slave uprising were discussed and ultimately rejected by the former slave Douglass, who thought its success unlikely. The October 1859 raid, which saw Brown and his several dozen followers seize control of the Harpers Ferry arsenal, ended in Brown's capture and hanging, and soon after, two of his followers were captured in Mount Alto (Franklin County) and Carlisle, also to be hanged for the attempted slave rebellion.[222]

John Brown's raid struck a nerve throughout the nation, becoming the hot topic of the coming presidential election in 1860, which would see Abraham Lincoln elevated to the Oval Office. However, neither Lincoln nor most of his fellow antislavery Republicans wished to associate themselves with the controversial abolitionist. Even Chambersburg's Republican paper, the *Franklin Repository*, tried to distance the town from Brown. "From what we have heard, it appears our Southern neighbors of Maryland and Virginia…are very indignant at the citizens of Chambersburg—regarding them as the most fanatical 'abolitionists' with which the country is troubled…Had our people had the least inkling of the designs of these deluded men they would have nipped the plot in the bud."[223]

The editors of the *Valley Spirit*, Chambersburg's Democratic paper, were astonished "that these men lived among us for months—transacted business through our Bank and Warehouses, kept up an extensive correspondence through our Post Office, and using the Telegraph occasionally and yet no one suspected their real character or designs. As incredible as this may seem, it is nevertheless true. Our community can scarcely be brought to realize it even now, and seem astounded at their own blindness. We feel very confident they have no aiders, abettors or sympathizers among us and this may account for our complete ignorance of their true object. They found none here to whom they could express their opinions or make known their intentions."[224]

Chapter Ten

CONFEDERATE INVASION

It was ten o'clock at night, on June 20, 1863, when the father and son team of Adam and J. Howard Wert heard "doleful cries and appeals for help…from the meadows adjacent." "In the meadows of my father's farm," a twenty-two-year-old J. Howard Wert and his father discovered "[a] colored family fleeing for safety and fearing capture, if overtaken by southern soldiers on the highways." They had attempted "to keep a course through the fields at some distance from the Baltimore Pike." In the darkness, they had stumbled upon what Wert himself termed a "labyrinth of waterways"—a triangular patch of field "enclosed on every side by deep water" flowing from two streams as well as a manmade mill run.

The entire area was "densely overgrown with a thicket of willows and bushes." The family that had found themselves entrapped within it was of unexpected size—a father, mother and no less than eleven children. As the Werts and their sympathizing neighbors pulled the large family from this nighttime watery abyss, they found themselves beholden by the luggage the family had brought with them. "They appeared to have prepared themselves for every eventuality for a life in the open," Wert wrote, "and probably, were actuated also by the desire to leave as little plunder as possible behind for the hated Confederates. Every member of this involuntary picnic party was loaded to full capacity, except the baby and the mother."

Among the load they carried were quilts, blankets, a featherbed, a ham, four loaves of "colossal size" bread, a frying skillet, a set each of tablespoons and teaspoons, knives and forks, a "much worn" butcher knife, a marriage certificate, a family Bible and even a framed portrait of Abraham Lincoln. Fortune had it that this family ended up in the hands of the Baltimore Pike's close-knit community of abolitionists, who, sensing the urgency, "promptly" sent the family toward the Susquehanna River, where they could cross and make for freedom across the river.[225]

South Central Pennsylvania's African American community in many cases became fugitives themselves when Robert E. Lee's Army of Northern Virginia made its way northward in June 1863. Once across the border, the Confederate legions spread themselves out in columns. To the east, a column of Confederates marched across the South Mountain, through Gettysburg and all the way to the banks of the Susquehanna at Wrightsville. Another force moved northward up the Cumberland Valley, through Shippensburg, Carlisle and the west shore, coming within a few miles of the state capital in Harrisburg. For the five thousand free African Americans living in Franklin, Cumberland, Adams and York Counties, the Confederate invasion spelled grave trouble.[226]

Reports were already circulating about what the Confederate vanguard was doing with free African Americans they encountered. Brigadier General Albert Gallatin Jenkins, a native Virginian, former congressman and slaveholding plantation owner, spearheaded the Confederate column northward up the Cumberland Valley. "One of the revolting features…was the scouring of the fields about town and searching of houses in portions of the place for negroes," recalled one Chambersburg resident. "[T]hose of them who had not fled upon the approach of the foe…sought concealment in the growing wheat fields about the town. Into these the cavalrymen rode in search of their prey, and many were caught—some after a desperate chase and being fired at."

Several African Americans were able to obtain freedom from Jenkins's Confederates through the influence and earnest application of friendly white citizens. Yet many were not so lucky. In Mercersburg, a longtime home to a large African American community, Dr. Philip Schaff penned in his diary as he watched "the poor negroes, the innocent cause of the war, are trembling like leaves and flying with their little bundles 'to the mountains,' especially, the numerous run-away slaves from Virginia, from fear of being captured as 'contrabands' and sold to the South." Many of those Schaff saw being shackled off into slavery down South were "such as I knew to have been born and raised on free soil."[227]

Many free blacks encountered assistance from longtime employers, such as Underground Railroad "conductor" Richard Woods. Visiting her grandfather's home near Carlisle, Nettie Jane Blair, Woods's young granddaughter, remembered waking up to a commotion one late June 1863 morning. "All the Negroes who had ever worked for grandfather had come down from the mountains with their belongings tied in bed quilts," she later recalled, and they "were gathering in the back yard. They were literally fed and then piled into big Conestoga wagons drawn by mules. Another wagon was stacked with food and then the whole outfit including the stock started for Harrisburg. Grandfather and his two sons James and Scott, headed this party and they were joined along the way by sympathetic friends and neighbors with their possessions."

The caravan crossed the Susquehanna "and went up into the Chester Valley where they rented barns and waited developments." Meanwhile, several of the women remained behind with two African Americans—one was "old Ag, the cook," and the other "a very good looking Mulatto girl" named Celie, who was serving as a nurse, and had been brought by the visiting girl and her mother from New York. "[B]oth Grandmother and Mother were greatly troubled [with] what to do with them," she reminisced, "for part of the program was to search the house and take off the Negroes. Finally they hit upon a plan to put a bed in the loft above the Spring House and hiding them there."

About half a dozen Confederates on horseback arrived at the Woods farm early the next morning. Nettie's mother watched as a Confederate horseman jumped a fence to scope out the neighboring meadow for any African Americans. "They all went all over the farm," Nettie recalled, "through the barn, and up the paddock." Most frightening was when the horsemen watered their mounts at the springhouse, while one of the African American women watched from within the springhouse. A close call, but they remained concealed and survived the encounter.[228]

In Shippensburg, Eunice Stewart found herself a prisoner in her own home. Occupying Confederates had "[e]very [s]treet and [a]lley in town" heavily guarded. She had reason to be concerned—her husband, Dr. Alexander Stewart, was an agent on the Underground Railroad and had left town before the Southern forces arrived. "I have four colored persons concealed in my house," Eunice confided on June 26. "We keep all the lower part locked and sit upstairs." As the days of the Confederate occupation wore on, she would continue to vent her anxieties with daily additions to a diary-style letter—which she would not mail until after the Confederates had departed.[229]

Within Gettysburg, Tillie Pierce Alleman watched as her African American neighbors fled the borough. She recalled:

This early twentieth-century photograph shows Richard D. Woods's springhouse, which the Woods family utilized as a hiding place for runaway slaves. In 1863, a black woman hid inside the springhouse as Confederate cavalrymen watered their mounts just inches away. *Cumberland County Historical Society.*

These folks mostly lived in the southwestern part of the town, and their flight was invariably down Breckenridge Street and Baltimore Street, and towards the woods on and around Culp's Hill. I can see them yet; men and women with bundles as large as old-fashioned feather ticks slung across their backs, almost bearing them to the ground. Children, also, carrying their bundles, and striving in vain to keep up with their seniors. The greatest consternation was depicted on all their countenances as they hurried along; crowding, and running against each other in their confusion; children stumbling, falling, and crying.[230]

Gettysburg's free black community, with seeds dating back to the late eighteenth century, was among the largest in South Central Pennsylvania. By 1860, there were 184 African Americans living in Gettysburg itself, while another 67 resided in neighboring Cumberland township. In the town of Gettysburg, the occupations of free blacks included day laborers, domestic servants, hostlers, cooks, blacksmiths, waiters, janitors, barbers, wagon makers and teamsters.

Owen Robinson was one of the 184 blacks who lived in Gettysburg. Robinson rented a house, where he resided with his family, and was both a "confectioner" and a janitor by trade. Charles McCurdy, a young Gettysburg boy, recalled him as "a well-to-do negro, who kept a little restaurant where he sold oysters in the winter and ice cream in [the] summer, and one of my delights as a boy, was to hang around his shop and watch the fascinating process of making the latter." Yet McCurdy routinely saw a dark truth behind this pleasant façade. "Whenever there was a report that the Rebels were coming," remembered Charles, Robinson would take off "with his family for a place of safety, and not return until the coast was clear...From the beginning of the war Owen had lived in [a] constant dread of being captured and taken south."[231]

On the corner of Breckenridge and Washington Streets once sat the home of Sydney O'Brien, the slave of James Gettys, founder and namesake of the town. Gettys would eventually free O'Brien and set her up in a home toward the southwestern end of the then infant town. Several decades later, the black community that grew up around it established St. Paul's African Methodist Episcopal Church on the site of O'Brien's home. Worshippers at St. Paul's AME soon after founded the Slaves' Refuge Society, which declared "it our indispensable duty to assist such of our brethren as shall come among us for the purpose of liberating themselves, and to raise all the means in our power to effect our object, which is to give liberty to our brethren groaning under the tyrannical yoke of oppression."[232]

In the surrounding farm fields and orchards that were Cumberland township, only two of the sixty-seven black residents were themselves farmers—most were day laborers. Those two men were Abraham Brien and Basil Biggs. Brien was nearing fifty-nine years old at the time of the Confederate invasion. He owned twenty acres of land, two small houses, a barn, a wagon shed and a corn crib. Despite the constant dangers, he had many ties to the area, which caused him to stay put in the turbulent borderland that was South Central Pennsylvania. His brother Moses lived in Gettysburg, his wife and children had been born in the state and his children attended nearby Granite Schoolhouse.

A short distance to the southwest, Basil Biggs was a tenant farmer along Marsh Creek. Forty-three years old, Biggs had been born in Maryland, but he lost his mother at an early age and was "bound out" for thirteen years of "very hard work." Once he reached adulthood, he traveled to Baltimore

Union patriotic envelopes addressed to the Biggs and Mathews families, free blacks living in Adams County. *J. Howard Wert Gettysburg Collection.*

and became a teamster and also met his wife, Mary Jackson. Basil and Mary had a home in Baltimore, but they soon faced an uphill battle to educate their children. For this reason, Biggs sold his property and in 1858 arrived in the Gettysburg area. A farmer in Cumberland township, at night Biggs guided fugitive slaves northward to Yellow Hill. Farther to the south, another African American, James Warfield owned thirteen acres, where he had his blacksmith shop. It was known as "a No. 1 stand, commanding a large and steady run of customers…one of the best blacksmith stands in the county."[233]

The looming threat of Confederate occupation forced Brien, Biggs and Warfield from their hard-earned homes and farmsteads, along with hundreds of other African Americans. Many blacks, however, remained in town when July 1, 1863, rolled around, and if they were not carefully concealed, were likely captured by the Confederate army. Countless residents fled never to return to Gettysburg again; others, like Brien, Biggs and Warfield, returned to a scene of devastation. James Warfield, whose farm had been headquarters for Confederate lieutenant general James Longstreet, lost two cattle and three hogs, along with countless fields of wheat and corn, pillaged fences and damage to his buildings, amounting to $516. Basil Biggs's homecoming quickly morphed into a nightmare, as he eyed nearly one hundred acres of wheat, oats, grass and corn destroyed and more than two dozen cattle, ten hogs and countless pieces of household furniture stolen, amounting to a total of $1,506 in damages. Attempting to ease the burden, Biggs found work removing bodies from the battlefield for reinternment in the newly formed National Cemetery.[234] For African Americans throughout South Central Pennsylvania, the Confederate invasion had proven to be yet another life-shattering ordeal.

Chapter Eleven

"GOD PLEAD MY CAUSE"

Lydia Hamilton Smith's roots ran deep in South Central Pennsylvania. A devout Catholic, Smith was born in the Adams County countryside to a white father and a mixed-race mother. As a young woman, she married Jacob Smith, a black barber with whom she had two sons. It was in her thirty-fifth year that Smith came to work for Congressman Thaddeus Stevens of Lancaster, formerly Gettysburg's state representative. Over the next several decades, Smith—by then a widow—would largely manage Stevens's domestic and business affairs in Lancaster, Gettysburg, Caledonia Furnace, Washington and wherever else Stevens was involved. As early as 1852, she was a property holder in Gettysburg, through Stevens's influence. And in the wake of the Battle of Gettysburg, Smith purchased a wagon load of food and clothing at her own expense, which she drove into town and distributed among the wounded.[235]

A glance at her personal belongings reveals a deep sense of spirituality, married with an unwavering sense of abolitionism. There is a hand-woven bookmark, depicting a bondsman down on one knee, constrained by shackles as he cries, "God Plead My Cause." Poems about freedom, liberty and equality—clipped from newspapers or periodicals—had clearly caught Smith's eye and heart. A beautifully decorated case contains the likeness of Smith—an ambrotype she had posed for while visiting Philadelphia. Within the elaborate case, her image is bounded on each side by an American flag, while an eagle nests overhead. The motto "E Pluribus Unum" floats upon a banner below her. Into this case, Smith deposited a small, hand-cut wafer, containing a

Bible verse: "For God shall bring every work into judgement, with every secret thing, whether it be good or whether it be evil."[236]

Smith was probably well acquainted with Edward McPherson, Gettysburg's two-term congressman. He was the great-grandson of Colonel Robert McPherson, the planter who once owned eleven slaves, and grandson of William McPherson, who owned multiple slaves well into the 1810s, including at least two who ran away. Edward was born in 1830 and around the age of twenty began studying law under Thaddeus Stevens in Lancaster. McPherson's rise was rapid, and before the decade was over, he was elected to Congress in 1858, representing a district spanning Adams, Franklin, Fulton, Bedford and Juniata Counties. When his district was altered for the 1862 election, McPherson lost his bid for a third term. However, as a loyal, antislavery Republican and close confidant of Stevens, McPherson remained in Washington. In December 1863, he was appointed clerk of the House of Representatives—a position that would place the Gettysburg native in a crucial role in the fight to abolish slavery.[237]

The man who defeated McPherson in 1862 was Democrat Archibald McAllister. Much like McPherson, McAllister's grandfather, also named Archibald McAllister, had operated a large plantation worked by several slaves. The elder Archibald McAllister, born in 1756, owned an extensive, three-hundred-plus-acre farm at Fort Hunter, just north of Harrisburg along the eastern banks of the Susquehanna. To an English traveler in 1794, McAllister was by far "the most spirited and intelligent farmer we had seen," deeming his property "a favourable specimen of an American plantation," with its carefully orchestrated crop rotation, manure use, thirty-acre orchard and distillery. To operate his expansive plantation and tavern, McAllister defied the spirit of Pennsylvania's gradual abolition, employing slave labor continuously until his 1831 death.

When Archibald McAllister journeyed to Lancaster to register his slaves in 1780, he laid claim to five men and women. Throughout the following decades, his force of slaves fluctuated. In November 1795, a twenty-eight-year-old slave named James fled the Fort Hunter plantation. James "speaks the English and German languages," McAllister described in a runaway ad, "chews tobacco, plays on the violin, [and] is fond of driving team." When financial difficulties struck Fort Hunter in the late 1820s, McAllister announced his intention "to dispose of all my colored people at private sale" in 1828. Circulated in the Harrisburg paper, McAllister offered sixty-one-year-old Sall Craig for sale, alongside three term slaves—twenty-eight- and twenty-two-year-old females and

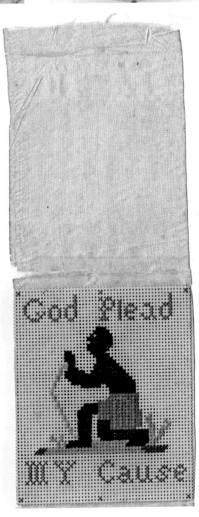

Above, left: An Adams County native, Lydia Hamilton Smith was employed for decades by Congressman Thaddeus Stevens, managing his business affairs throughout central Pennsylvania and in Washington. This ambrotype, taken in Philadelphia, shows Smith's passionate patriotism for her country, featuring a gold backing adorned with American flags and bayonets. Smith was a mixed-race woman, sometimes referred to as a "quadroon" and other times a "mulatto." *J. Howard Wert Gettysburg Collection.*

Above, right: This locket-sized daguerreotype shows the attributed mother of Lydia Hamilton Smith. *J. Howard Wert Gettysburg Collection.*

Right: This hand-woven bookmark belonged to Lydia Hamilton Smith. Its message, "God Plead My Cause," is a clear indication of both Smith's deep sense of faith and of her heartfelt devotion to the abolition of slavery. *J. Howard Wert Gettysburg Collection.*

a twenty-four-year-old male. Sall, a slave for life who had been with McAllister at least back to 1780, decided to flee her master of fifty-odd years as soon as she caught wind of his intent to sell her.

The proprietor's grandson was born at Fort Hunter in 1813. The younger Archibald McAllister thus entered life on one of Pennsylvania's last remaining slave plantations. He later moved to Blair County, where he was a manufacturer of iron, and in 1862 won his lone term in Congress, defeating Edward McPherson.[238] McAllister entered the halls of Congress in a crucial time in American history, and his term was filled with heated discussion over the proposed Thirteenth Amendment, which would abolish slavery nationwide. The Senate overwhelmingly adopted the amendment in April 1864, but when the question came before the House two months later, McAllister was among those who successfully voted to block it. However, when the amendment returned to the House floor in January 1865, the Pennsylvanian had a change of heart.[239] Against

Top: A modern-day view of the African American cemetery near Fort Hunter. *Photo by the author.*

Bottom: The grave of Andrew Craig features a hand pointing up toward heaven. Born in 1795, Andrew served as a term slave, possibly into the 1820s, before gaining his freedom. *Photo by the author.*

his party's will, Archibald McAllister voted yes, a vote that was recorded by House clerk Edward Mcpherson.

The ballot cast by Congressman Archibald McAllister was one of the deciding votes in the passage of the Thirteenth Amendment. By December 1865, it had been ratified by enough states to become a reality. The abolition of slavery achieved in 1865 was the realization of the long-held dreams of men who joined the Adams County Protection Society some forty-five years before and the Adams County Anti-Slavery Society in 1836, twenty-nine years earlier. For others, like William Wright and Daniel Kaufman, the abolition of slavery was a vindication of their unlawful participation in the Underground Railroad. Yet for Edward McPherson and Archibald McAllister, the Thirteenth Amendment was a way to bury the hatchet of their families' slaveholding pasts and, regardless of their politics, come together for the good of the nation.

Sall Craig's family remained at Fort Hunter—no longer slaves, they would continue to work on and near the plantation to make ends meet. On a hillside overlooking Fort Hunter and the Susquehanna River, the Craig family ordained a quiet location for their family burial grounds. They gathered stones from the surrounding mountainside for a modest stone wall, enclosing their small lot. Under the shade of a towering locust tree, the Craig family would lay their husbands, wives, brothers and sisters to rest—gazing out at the rising mountains to the north and west—free at last.

NOTES

Chapter One

1. Sturtevant, *Harrisburg Directory*, 6.
2. *American Weekly Mercury*, October 29–November 5, 1741; Rupp, *History and Topography*, 226–27; "Harris Trading Post Interpretation," Harris Trading Post File, Historical Society of Dauphin County. Hereinafter cited as HSDC.
3. Volwiler, *George Croghan*, 26–48; Wainwright, *George Croghan*, 4–13.
4. Rupp, *History and Topography*, 226–27; Egle, *Notes and Queries*, 37–38; Sturtevant, *Harrisburg Directory*, 6; *Harrisburg Telegraph*, "John Harris," June 10, 1912; George W. Harris, "A Historical Sketch," newspaper clippings, Hercules File, HSDC.
5. John Harris Will, John Harris Sr. Will File, HSDC; Harris, "A Historical Sketch"; *Harrisburg Telegraph*, "John Harris."
6. Egle, *Notes and Queries*, 38; According to early descendants of John Harris, Hercules and two of his children were buried beside his one-time master, beneath the mulberry tree. See William M. Awl to George W. Harris, July 12, 1859, Hercules File, HSDC.
7. Volwiler, *George Croghan*, 48; Wainwright, *George Croghan*, 10, 44.

Chapter Two

8. Davis, *Problem of Slavery*, 303–04.
9. Lemon, *Best Poor Man's Country*, 2–13.

10. Davis, *Problem of Slavery*, 292–95, 303–04; Brown, "Pennsylvania's Antislavery Pioneers," 73–74.

11. Wax, "Africans on the Delaware," 39.

12. Ibid., 38–47; Davis, *Problem of Slavery*, 304–05; Tully, "Patterns of Slaveholding," 284–97; Wax, "Quaker Merchants," 145; Wax, "Demand for Slave Labor," 337–39; Wax, "Negro Imports," 254–60.

13. Fox, *Gospel Family Order*, 16, 18.

14. Nash and Soderlund, *Freedom by Degrees*, 41–47.

15. Vaux, *Memoirs*, 1–20.

Chapter Three

16. Wax, "Demand for Slave Labor," 331–45; Wax, "Negro Imports," 259; Tully, "Patterns of Slaveholding," 287–94.

17. *Pennsylvania Gazette*, June 29, 1749.

18. Tully, "Patterns of Slaveholding," 294–96; Wax, "Africans on the Delaware," 38–47; Wax, "Negro Imports," 256.

19. Churchman, *Account of the Gospel Labours*, 175–76.

20. Gummere, *Journal and Essays*, 161–62.

21. Nash and Soderlund, *Freedom by Degrees*, 51–57.

22. Greene and Harrington, *American Population*, 117.

23. Robert Dunning, will dated 1750, Book A-1, Cumberland County Register of Wills, Carlisle, PA.

24. John Williamson, will dated May 21, 1757, Book A-43, Register of Wills.

25. John Blair, will dated February 13, 1769, Book B-21-23, Register of Wills.

26. Philip Davis, will dated May 15, 1753, Book A-71-74, Register of Wills.

27. Henry P. Pawling Estate Inventory, 1763, P-005, microfilm at Cumberland County Historical Society, Carlisle, PA. Hereinafter cited as CCHS.

28. Present-day Middlesex township.

29. Robert Callendar Estate Inventory, August 19, 1776, C-036, microfilm at CCHS; Robert Callendar, will, Will Book I-164, Allegheny County Register of Wills; East Pennsborough and Middleton township Tax Records, 1765–1773, transcripts at CCHS; Cumberland County Clerk of Courts. Slave Returns: 1780.081 (Frances Callendar). Cumberland County Archives, Carlisle, PA. Hereinafter cited as Slave Returns, CCA.

30. Cumberland County Tax Records, 1765, transcripts at CCHS; Due to a lack of slave and indentured servant records for East Pennsborough, Hamilton, Fannett or Peters township in the 1765 tax records, for this tally I supplemented the figures available for the following year, 1766,

excepting for Fannett. The earliest available documentation for Fannett is 1768. Comparisons with other townships demonstrate that slave levels remained very steady throughout the late 1760s.

31. *Pennsylvania Gazette,* July 27, 1749.
32. Ibid., October 13, 1763.
33. Ibid., August 30, 1770.
34. Ibid., October 11, 1764.
35. Ibid., October 11, 1764, August 30, 1770.
36. *Dauphin Oracle,* December 8, 1794.
37. *Pennsylvania Gazette,* July 13, 1769.
38. Ibid., May 26, 1773.

Chapter Four

39. Dr. John Calhoon Estate Inventory, 1783, C-053, microfilm at CCHS; Slave Returns, Jonathan Calhoon, CCA; Hopewell and Guilford township Tax Records, 1770–1779, transcripts at CCHS; Warner, Beers and Company, *History of Franklin County,* 272, 473.
40. Jenkins, "Fragments of a Journal," 5:63–64.
41. Nash and Soderlund, *Freedom by Degrees,* 4–5, 71, 89.
42. The 1770 numbers are drawn in a similar fashion as those from 1765. The 1770 tax records for Hopewell township are partly missing, so the extant number from 1769 is included in this count.
43. Cumberland County Tax Records, 1770–1775, transcripts at CCHS.
44. Ibid., 1775, 1778.
45. *Pennsylvania Archives,* Series 3, 21:3–169.
46. *Pennsylvania Gazette,* February 7, 1778; These runaway ads come from the brief period (December 1777–June 1778) when the *Pennsylvania Gazette* was printed in York, due to the British occupation of Philadelphia.
47. Ibid., February 28, 1778.
48. Ibid., February 14, 1778.
49. Ibid., March 21, 1778.
50. Bill of Sale, Patrick Jack to John Finley, December 22, 1788, Box 9, Folder 11, CCHS.
51. Bill of Sale, Jacob Gilleylen to Robert Whitehill, November 5, 1770, Folder 9, Box 2B, Robert Whitehill Papers, CCHS.
52. Bill of Sale, John Kirpatrick to Joseph Spear, November 30, 1774, 1–29, CCHS.

53. Nash and Soderlund, *Freedom by Degrees*, 12–13, 99.

54. Konkle, *George Bryan*, 189–99.

55. *Pennsylvania Archives*, Series 3 21:3–169; Gibson, *History of York County*, 317.

56. Tax records 1779–1780.

57. Nash and Soderlund, *Freedom by Degrees*, 102–03.

58. *Journals of the House of Representatives*, 434–36.

59. Ibid., 436.

60. Nash and Soderlund, *Freedom by Degrees*, 99, 111.

61. Alosi, *Shadow of Freedom*, 19–20; Gibson, *History of York County*, 317.

62. "Philotheukos," *Pennsylvania Packet*, December 2, 1780; Brunhouse, *Counter-Revolution in Pennsylvania*, 102; Nash and Soderlund, *Freedom by Degrees*, 112–13.

Chapter Five

63. Brodsky, *Benjamin Rush*, 9–27, 81–83, 147–50, 220.

64. Benjamin Rush to Barbeu Dobourg, April 29, 1773, in Butterfield, *Letters of Benjamin Rush*, 1:76–77.

65. Benjamin Rush to Jeremy Belknap, August 19, 1788, in Butterfield, *Letters of Benjamin Rush*, 1:481–83.

66. Benjamin Rush to John Armstrong, March 19, 1783, in Butterfield, *Letters of Benjamin Rush*, 1:294–97.

67. Butterfield, "Rush's Journal," 443–56.

68. Benjamin Rush to Charles Nisbet, April 19, 1784, in Butterfield, *Letters of Benjamin Rush*, 1:321–25.

69. Charles Nisbet to Lord Buchan, April 20, 1786, in Miller, *Memoir of the Reverend Charles Nisbet*, 144.

70. Benjamin Rush to John Adams, July 13, 1812, in Butterfield, *Letters of Benjamin Rush*, 2:1150; Brodsky, *Benjamin Rush*, 309, 381; Benjamin Rush to Mrs. Rush, August 22, 1787, in Butterfield, *Letters of Benjamin Rush*, 1:436–37; Butterfield, "Rush's Journal," 443–56.

71. Slave Returns, James Pollock, CCA; Cumberland County Clerk of Courts. Slaveholder Register (2 vols.), James Pollock, Cumberland County Archives, Carlisle, PA; Benjamin Rush to Jeremy Belknap, August 19, 1788, in Butterfield, *Letters of Benjamin Rush*, 1:481–83.

72. Slave Returns, John Montgomery, CCA; Slaveholder Register, John Montgomery, CCA.

73. Butterfield, "Rush's Journal," 443–56.

74. James Pollock, will dated September 26, 1790, Book F-239-240, Cumberland County Register of Wills, Carlisle, PA; Slaveholder Register, James Pollock, CCA.

75. Slaveholder Register, John Montgomery, CCA.

76. *Carlisle Gazette*, June 13, 1787; The female child alluded to is almost certainly Phillis or Patience.

77. John Montgomery, will dated September 18, 1800, Book G-340-341, Cumberland County Register of Wills, Carlisle, PA.

78. Butterfield, "Rush's Journal," 443–56.

79. Ibid.; Slaveholder Register, Robert Magaw, CCA.

80. *Pennsylvania Archives*, Series 3, 21:666; Butterfield, "Rush's Journal," 443–56.

81. Benjamin Rush to John Montgomery, October 15, 1782, September 1, 1783, November 13, 1784, in Butterfield, *Letters of Benjamin Rush*, 1:290–91, 309–10, 341–44; Warner, Beers and Company, *History of Cumberland and Adams Counties*, 3:364–65; *Pennsylvania Archives*, Series 3, 21:740.

82. For an excellent study examining this social phenomenon, see McCoy, "Forgetting Freedom," 141–70.

83. "An Act to Explain and Amend an Act Entitled 'An Act for the Gradual Abolition of Slavery,'" Pennsylvania, *Statutes at Large*, 13:52–56; Zilversmit, *First Emancipation*, 158–59.

84. "An Act for the Gradual Abolition of Slavery," Pennsylvania, *Statutes at Large*, 10:67–73.

85. Slave Returns, George Stevenson, CCA.

86. Slave Returns, Francis Campbell, CCA.

87. Slave Returns, Henry Pawling, CCA; Antrim township Tax Records, 1780, transcript at CCHS.

88. Henry P. Pawling Estate Inventory, 1763, P-005, microfilm at CCHS.

89. Pennsylvania, *Statutes at Large*, 11:470.

90. Thomas Poe Estate Inventory, 1770, P-011, microfilm at CCHS; Poe's will (also in 1770) lists two slaves bequeathed to his wife, however, instead of a Negro man as stated in the inventory, the will reports "one Negro Wench named Nan and one Negro Boy named Peter." See Thomas Poe, will dated September 3, 1770, Book B-63, Cumberland County Register of Wills, Carlisle, PA.

91. Carlisle borough Tax Records, 1770, transcript at CCHS; Charles Pattison Estate Inventory, 1771, P-012, microfilm at CCHS.

92. Data drawn from both the Slave Returns and Slaveholder Register, CCA.

93. Ibid.

94. Ibid.

95. *Pennsylvania Archives*, Series 3, 21:659–61.
96. Benjamin Rush to Richard Price, October 15, 1785, in Butterfield, *Letters of Benjamin Rush*, 1:371–73.
97. McCoy, "Forgetting Freedom," 141–70.
98. *Carlisle Gazette*, August 2, 1786.
99. *Carlisle Gazette*, July 15, 1789.
100. Belles Lettres Society Minute Book, August 12, 1786, Archives and Special Collections, Dickinson College.
101. Ibid., November 24, 1787
102. Ibid., July 11, 1789; Morrow, *History of Warren County*, 357–60.
103. Belles Lettres Society Minute Book, July 26, 1794, August 9, 1794, Dickinson College.
104. Benjamin Rush, "To the Pennsylvania Abolition Society," January 14, 1795, in Butterfield, *Letters of Benjamin Rush*, 2:756–59.
105. Long, *History of Jamaica*, 2:351–52.
106. Benjamin Rush to Thomas Jefferson, February 4, 1797, in Butterfield, *Letters of Benjamin Rush*, 2:785–86.

Chapter Six

107. "To the inhabitants of the borough of York and its vicinity to the distance of 10 miles," March 21, 1803, slavery file, York County Heritage Trust. Hereinafter cited as YCHT.
108. Bureau of the Census, *Heads of Families*, 8:8–11, 75–86, 112–21, 269–92; Beard had registered ten slaves in 1780. See Slaveholder Register, Richard Beard, CCA.
109. Petition of Jube Harris, September 10, 1816, Insolvent Debtors Petitions, Cumberland County Archives, Carlisle, PA.
110. Petition of Francis Smith, June 30, 1818, Insolvent Debtors Petitions, Cumberland County Archives, Carlisle, PA.
111. Petition of Richard Sanders, August 8, 1825, Insolvent Debtors Petitions, Cumberland County Archives, Carlisle, PA.
112. Petition of Samuel Howard, April 10, 1826, Insolvent Debtors Petitions, Cumberland County Archives, Carlisle, PA.
113. Petition of Thomas Early, August 8, 1825, Insolvent Debtors Petitions, Cumberland County Archives, Carlisle, PA.
114. Petition of John Coleman, August 13, 1827, Insolvent Debtors Petitions, Cumberland County Archives, Carlisle, PA.

115. Petition of John Coleman, August 30, 1831, Insolvent Debtors Petitions, Cumberland County Archives, Carlisle, PA.

116. Poorhouse Director's Statement, April 1814, Cumberland County Archives, Carlisle, PA.

117. Newspaper clippings, *Pennsylvania Herald and York General Advertiser*, January–October 1789, slavery file, YCHT. This advertisement is dated February 24, 1789.

118. Jennet Grier to John Madison, Bill of Sale, April 24, 1809, slavery file, YCHT.

119. William Brown Parker to James Hamilton, October 27, 1811, James Hamilton Papers, MG 34-17, CCHS; For prior attempts to purchase a slave from Philadelphia, see Cranston & Alexander to James Hamilton, June 26, 1798, James Hamilton Papers, MG 33-10, CCHS; James Hamilton to John Brown, December 13, [1802], Sylvester B. Sadler Collection, MG 16-18, CCHS; John Brown to James Hamilton, January 14, 1803, and July 15, 1803, James Hamilton Papers, MG 34-2, CCHS.

120. William Brown Parker to James Hamilton, November 22, 1811, James Hamilton Papers, MG 34-17, CCHS.

121. Ibid., December 12, 1811.

122. Ibid., December 20, 1811.

123. Ibid., December 28, 1811; January 31, 1812.

124. *Carlisle Gazette*, September 7, 1785.

125. Ibid., May 21, 1794.

126. Newspaper clippings, YCHT. This advertisement is dated January 7, 1789.

127. Ibid.; This advertisement is dated January 26, 1789.

128. *Carlisle Gazette*, May 21, 1794.

129. *York Recorder*, March 30, 1811.

130. *Carlisle Gazette*, August 13, 1794.

131. *Farmers' Register*, October 10, 1798.

132. Ibid., May 23, 1798.

133. Ibid., June 20, 1798.

134. Ibid., August 29, 1798.

135. Ibid., February 6, 1799.

136. *Carlisle Gazette*, November 30, 1785.

137. Turner, *Negro in Pennsylvania*, 99–100; McCoy, "Forgetting Freedom," 141–70.

138. Thomas Fisher Petition, November 5, 1806, Indentured Servant and Apprentice Matters, Cumberland County Clerk of Courts, Carlisle, PA; Slave Returns, Thomas Fisher, CCA.

139. Slave Returns, William Kelso, CCA.
140. Carothers sale papers regarding Cloe, Box 9-15, CCHS.
141. For the various reports and trial excerpts of the Chloe case, see *Carlisle Gazette*, June 10 and 24, July 15 and 22, 1801; Chloe's confession (*Carlisle Gazette*, July 22, 1801) is significant, as it provides one of the only known accounts from a South Central Pennsylvania slave.
142. *Carlisle Gazette*, July 22, 1801.
143. Pennsylvania, *Minutes of the Supreme Executive Council*, 25:475–77; McCauley, *Historical Sketch*, 59.
144. *Carlisle Gazette*, November 27, 1793.
145. Slave Returns, William Allison, CCA.
146. *Pennsylvania Herald and York General Advertiser*, June 18, 1794.
147. *Dauphin Oracle*, January 11, 1797.
148. Slave Returns, John Williams, CCA.
149. *Carlisle Gazette*, June 24, 1801.
150. Ibid., July 11, 1804.
151. *Adams Centinel*, June 5, 1805. William McPherson is listed in 1783, alongside his father and brother, as owning three slaves. (See *Pennsylvania Archives*, Series 3, 21:740).
152. Ibid., September 16, 1818.
153. Ibid., July 25, 1810.

Chapter 7

154. Ibid., January 10, 1821.
155. Ibid., April 9, 1823.
156. Newspaper clippings, YCHT. This advertisement is dated February 24, 1789.
157. *Adams Centinel*, June 12, 1805.
158. Ibid., August 1, 1810.
159. Ibid., December 11, 1805.
160. Ibid., January 10, 1821.
161. Smith, *On the Edge of Freedom*, 19–22.
162. Ibid., 18–22.
163. *Pennsylvania Herald and York General Advertiser*, June 18, 1794.
164. *Adams Centinel*, November 22, 1820.
165. Ibid.
166. Smith, *On the Edge of Freedom*, 19–22.

167. Clay, "Speech before American Colonization Society," January 20, 1827, in *Papers of Henry Clay* (6:92–94, 96); "Speech of Mr. Clay," 134–35, *Niles' Weekly Register*, October 29, 1842.
168. "Constitution of the Cumberland county Colonization Society," Pamphlet File P 2-5, CCHS.
169. *Adams Centinel*, April 9, 1818.
170. Ibid., December 25, 1822.
171. Ibid., January 20, 1819; January 9, 1823.
172. Ibid., January 9, 1822.
173. Bureau of the Census, *Heads of Families*, 8:8–11; Bureau of the Census, *Return of the Whole Number of Persons*, 43–48; Bureau of the Census, *Aggregate Amount*, 39–41.
174. McCoy, "Forgetting Freedom," 141–70.
175. Examination of the Slaveholder Register, CCA.
176. Register of Negroes and Mulattoes, 1800–1820. Adams County Prothonotary, Gettysburg, PA.
177. Bill of sale, "a certain Negro Girl named 'Esther,'" sold by Esther Brisben to Jacob M. Haldeman, MG 64 Haldeman-Wright Family Collection, Box 1, Folder 4, Pennsylvania State Archives.
178. William Bryson Estate Inventory, October 29, 1818, noted in Jeremiah Zeamer Notebook, 40-7, CCHS.
179. Slave Returns, Matthew Loudon, CCA; Slaveholder Register, Matthew Loudon, CCA; Matthew Loudon's Will, in Jeremiah Zeamer Notebook, 40-7, CCHS.
180. Slave marriage, December 2, 1806, Zeamer Notebook, 40-7, CCHS.
181. Bolin, "Slaveholders and Slaves of Adams County," 9:58.

Chapter Eight

182. Seward, *William H. Seward*, 165–66.
183. Examination of the Slaveholder Register, CCA; Bureau of the Census, *Census for 1820*, 87–93; Bureau of the Census, *Abstract of the Returns*, 12–13; Bureau of the Census, *Compendium of the Enumeration of the Inhabitants*, 26. Evidently, census takers for the 1820 census only counted slaves for life and not term slaves. This was a common practice, also occurring during the Septennial Census (such as 1807). For slaves, the 1820 census lists Adams County with twenty-three slaves; Franklin, nineteen; Cumberland, seventeen; and York, six—all of whom were either in the twenty-six to

forty-five age category, or "45 and upwards" category, with respect to age. Not included in this tally were a wealth of younger, term slaves who remained in a temporary state of bondage. In the 1830 census, it is more difficult to ascertain who was counted; Adams County held forty-five slaves; Cumberland, seven; Franklin, eleven; and York, twenty-eight.

184. *Adams Centinel,* January 31, 1827.

185. Ibid., December 23, 1829.

186. Nash and Soderlund, *Freedom by Degrees,* 111.

187. Indenture, Jacob to William D. Seymour, March 25, 1839, Container 008-1, Folder 17b, CCHS; Also see Indenture, "Negroe Richard" to Isaac Brown Parker, May 6, 1811, Container 8, Folder 18, CCHS.

188. Wert, *Episodes of Gettysburg,* 92–93.

189. Ibid., 29.

190. Trefousse, *Thaddeus Stevens,* 12–36; Smedley, *History of the Underground Railroad,* 36; Thaddeus Stevens File, Adams County Historical Society; *Adams Centinel,* October 22, 1817; Smith, *On the Edge of Freedom,* 22–23; Wert, *Episodes of Gettysburg,* 27.

191. *Star and Republican Banner,* July 11, 1836.

192. Ibid.

193. Ibid.

194. Ibid.

195. The proceedings were printed in the *Star and Republican Banner* on September 26, 1836, but can be found reprinted in Wert, *Episodes of Gettysburg,* 23–27.

196. Wert, *Episodes of Gettysburg,* 30–34.

197. Ibid., 39–48; Minute Book, "Minutes of the Adams County A. Slavery Society," J. Howard Wert Gettysburg Collection (hereinafter cited as JHWGC); Joel Wierman to Adam Wert, August 6, 1837, JHWGC; Huldah Justice to Adam Wert, August 16, 1837, JHWGC; Allen Robinette to Adam Wert, January 27, 1839, JHWGC; William Jay, *A View of the Action of the Federal Government, in behalf of Slavery* (New York: American Antislavery Society, 1839), original marked copy in JHWGC.

Chapter Nine

198. Pennington, *Fugitive Blacksmith,* 14–42; Webber, *American to the Backbone,* 1–40; Still, *Still's Underground Railroad Records,* 692.

199. Wert, *Episodes of Gettysburg,* 29, 92–93; Pennington, *Fugitive Blacksmith,* 43.

200. See McCauslin, *Reconstructing the Past.*

201. Pennington, *Fugitive Blacksmith*, 42.

202. Ibid., 42–49.

203. Ibid., xii-xiv; Webber, *American to the Backbone*, 34.

204. S.R. McAllister to J. Howard Wert, December 2, 1904, JHWGC; Smith, *On the Edge of Freedom*, 27–28.

205. Drew, *North-Side View of Slavery*, 116.

206. Hiram E. Wertz, "A paper read on 'The Underground Railway' before the Hamilton Library Association, of Carlisle, Penna.,' on the evening of the 24th of February 1911," typescript, MG 72, Folder 7a, CCHS; Anderson, *Presbyterianism: Its Relation to the Negro*, 155; Keefner, McCulloh and Stenger, *Tuscarora Reader*, 89; Vermilyea, "Effect of Lee's Invasion"; "Title of Dobbin House."

207. Smith, *On the Edge of Freedom*, 32–34; Basil Biggs Obituary, *Gettysburg Compiler*, June 13, 1906; Switala, *Underground Railroad in Pennsylvania*, 103–11; Wertz, "A paper read on 'The Underground Railway,'" typescript, MG 72, Folder 7a, CCHS; Vermilyea, "Effect of Lee's Invasion"; Blockson, *Underground Railroad in Pennsylvania*, 142–47.

208. Wert, *Episodes of Gettysburg*, 53–55, 58–59, 67–72.

209. Theodore McAllister's account, which was originally published in the *Miller's Review* of March 15, 1912, can also be found reprinted in Wert, *Episodes of Gettysburg*, 54–55.

210. Robert Toombs to My Dear Julia, August 24, 25, 1850, Robert Toombs Papers, Hargrett Rare Book and Manuscript Library, University of Georgia; S.R. McAllister to J. Howard Wert, December 2, 1904, JHWGC; Siebert, *Underground Railroad*, 174–76.

211. Underground Railroad file, YCHT; Switala, *Underground Railroad*, 121–22.

212. Eunice Stewart to My Dear Parents, June 25, 1863, JHWGC; Notes on Samuel Taylor, Jeremiah Zeamer Papers, 40-7, CCHS; Switala, *Underground Railroad*, 104–11.

213. "Tumult and Riot," *Carlisle Herald*, June 9, 1847; "The Riot Trial," *American Volunteer*, September 2, 1847; "To the Public," Carlisle *American Volunteer*, October 14, 1847; Slotten, "McClintock Slave Riot," 14–33.

214. Tritt and Watt, *At a Place Called the Boiling Springs*, 111–17.

215. Jeremiah Zeamer Notes, 40-7, CCHS.

216. "A Hard Case," *Pennsylvania Freeman*, December 22, 1853; Tritt and Watt, *At a Place Called the Boiling Springs*, 111–17.

217. Nettie Jane Blair Reminisce, 1934, Box 120-13, CCHS; Sharp, *Biographical Annals*, 764–65; John Albert Shugart Jr., "The Underground Railroad in Cumberland County 1840 to 1860," mss. in MG 72, CCHS.

218. Minot, *Statutes at Large*, 9:462–65.

219. S.R. McAllister to J. Howard Wert, December 2, 1904, JHWGC.

220. Smedley, *History of the Underground Railroad*, 36–45; Wert, *Episodes of Gettysburg*, 94.

221. "Daring Abduction of Negroes," *Carlisle American*, June 15, 1859; "The Kidnappers," *Carlisle American*, June 22, 1859; Sharp, *Biographical Annals*, 765; Warner, Beers and Company, *History of Cumberland and Adams Counties*, 222.

222. For further details, see Smith, *On the Edge of Freedom*, 154–56.

223. *Franklin Repository*, October 26, 1859.

224. *Chambersburg Valley Spirit*, October 26, 1859.

Chapter Ten

225. Wert, *Episodes of Gettysburg*, 105–06; Wert considered this his "last trip on Gettysburg's Underground Railroad."

226. Kennedy, *Population of the United States*, 406–39; African American populations were almost certainly undercounted by census takers, and therefore 5,000 could be said to be a fairly conservative number. Franklin County had 1,799 according to the census of 1860, Cumberland 1,340, Adams 474 and York 1,366.

227. Hoke, *Great Invasion*, 96, 107–08.

228. Nettie Jane Blair Reminisce, 1934, Box 120-13, CCHS.

229. Eunice Stewart to My Dear Parents, June 25, 1863, JHWGC.

230. Alleman, *At Gettysburg*, 19–20.

231. 1860 U.S. Census, Borough of Gettysburg and Cumberland Township, Population Schedule, National Archives and Records Administration microfilm M653; McCurdy, *Gettysburg*, 19–20.

232. Vermilyea, "Effect of Lee's Invasion"; Smith, *On the Edge of Freedom*, 28–29.

233. Basil Biggs Obituary, *Gettysburg Compiler*, June 13, 1906; Vermilyea, "Effect of Lee's Invasion"; Gettysburg's African-American Community File, GNMP.

234. James Warfield, Basil Biggs, Petitions, Civilian Claims Files, GNMP; Vermilyea, "Effect of Lee's Invasion."

Chapter Eleven

235. Trefousse, *Thaddeus Stevens*, 46, 69; Brodie, *Thaddeus Stevens*, 86–93; *Star and Banner*, August 6, 1863; Deed, Anthony Codori to Ann Maria Taylor, April 15, 1864, Deed W-410, Adams County Historical Society. In 1837, the property in Gettysburg was sold to Stevens, who in 1852 "conveyed" it to Smith, who then sold it in 1856.

236. Smith's artifacts survive as part of the J. Howard Wert Gettysburg Collection.

237. Warner, Beers and Company, *History of Cumberland and Adams Counties*, 3:364–65.

238. "Register of Negroe and Mulatto Slaves & Servants 1780," Lancaster County History; *Dauphin Oracle*, November 9, 1795; *Pennsylvania Republican and Democratic Herald*, December 26, 1828; McAllister, *Descendants of Archibald McAllister*; Cooper, *Letters from America*, 123–35.

239. *Congressional Globe*, 38th Congress, 1st Session, 2995; *Congressional Globe*, 38th Congress, 2nd Session, 531.

BIBLIOGRAPHY

Books and Articles

Alleman, Tillie Pierce. *At Gettysburg: Or, What a Girl Saw and Heard of the Battle.* New York: W. Lake Borland, 1889.

Alosi, John. *Shadow of Freedom: Slavery in Post-Revolutionary Cumberland County, 1780–1810.* Shippensburg, PA: Shippensburg University, 2001.

Anderson, Matthew. *Presbyterianism: Its Relation to the Negro.* Philadelphia: John McGill White, 1897.

Blockson, Charles L. *The Underground Railroad in Pennsylvania.* Jacksonville, NC: Charles Blockson, 1981.

Bolin, Larry C. "Slaveholders and Slaves of Adams County." *Adams County History* (2003).

Brodie, Fawn M. *Thaddeus Stevens: Scourge of the South.* New York: W.W. Norton, 1959.

Brodsky, Alyn. *Benjamin Rush: Patriot and Physician.* New York: St. Martin's, 2004.

Brown, Ira V. "Pennsylvania's Antislavery Pioneers, 1688–1776." *Pennsylvania History* 55, no. 2 (April 1988).

Brunhouse, Robert L. *The Counter-Revolution in Pennsylvania, 1776–1790.* Harrisburg: Pennsylvania Historical and Museum Commission, 1971.

Butterfield, L.H. "Dr. Benjamin Rush's Journal of a Trip to Carlisle in 1784." *Pennsylvania Magazine of History and Biography* 74, no. 4 (October 1950).

———, ed. *Letters of Benjamin Rush.* 2 vols. London: Oxford University Press, 1951.

Churchman, John. *An Account of the Gospel Labours, and Christian Experiences of a Faithful Minister of Christ, John Churchman.* Philadelphia: Joseph Crukshank, 1779.

Clay, Henry. *The Papers of Henry Clay.* 10 vols. Lexington: University of Kentucky, 1959–1991.

Cooper, Thomas. *Letters from America to a Friend in England.* London: J. Johnson, 1795.

Davis, David Brion. *The Problem of Slavery in Western Culture.* New York: Oxford University Press, 1966.

Drew, Benjamin. *The North-Side View of Slavery; The Refugee: or the Narratives of Fugitive Slaves in Canada.* Boston: John P. Jewett, 1856.

Egle, William Henry, ed. *Notes and Queries: Historical, Biographical and Genealogical Relating Chiefly to Interior Pennsylvania.* Harrisburg, PA: Harrisburg Publishing Company, 1901.

[Fox, George]. *Gospel Family Order, Being a Short Discourse concerning the Ordering of Families, both of Whites, Blacks and Indians.* N.p., 1676.

Gibson, John, ed. *History of York County Pennsylvania, From the Earliest Period to the Present Time.* Chicago: F.A. Battey, 1886.

Greene, Evarts B., and Virginia D. Harrington. *American Population before the Federal Census of 1790.* New York: Columbia University Press, 1932.

Gummere, Amelia Mott, ed. *The Journal and Essays of John Woolman.* New York: MacMillan Company, 1922.

Hoke, Jacob. *The Great Invasion of 1863.* Dayton, OH: W.J. Shuey, 1887.

Jenkins, Howard M. "Fragments of a Journal Kept by Samuel Foulke." *Pennsylvania Magazine of History and Biography* (1881).

Keefner, Nancy, Joan McCulloh and Betty Stenger, eds. *The Tuscarora Reader.* Mercersburg, PA: Mercersburg Historical Society, 2000.

Konkle, Burton Alva. *George Bryan and the Constitution of Pennsylvania, 1731–1791.* Philadelphia: William J. Campbell, 1922.

Lemon, James T. *The Best Poor Man's Country: A Geographical Study of Early Southeastern Pennsylvania.* Baltimore: Johns Hopkins Press, 1972.

Long, Edward. *The History of Jamaica, Or, General Survey of the Ancient and Modern State of That Island.* London: T. Lowndes, 1774.

McAllister, Mary Catherine. *Descendants of Archibald McAllister.* Harrisburg, PA: Scheffer, 1898.

McCauley, I.H. *Historical Sketch of Franklin County, Pennsylvania.* Chambersburg, PA: D.F. Pursel, 1878.

McCauslin, Debra Sandoe. *Reconstructing the Past: Puzzle of the Lost Community at Yellow Hill.* Gettysburg, PA: For the Cause Productions, 2007.

McCoy, Michael. "Forgetting Freedom: White Anxiety, Black Presence, and Gradual Abolition in Cumberland County, Pennsylvania, 1780–1838." *Pennsylvania Magazine of History and Biography* 136, no. 2 (April 2012).

McCurdy, Charles M. *Gettysburg: A Memoir.* Pittsburgh: Reed & Writing Company, 1929.

Miller, Samuel, ed. *Memoir of the Reverend Charles Nisbet, D.D. Late President of Dickinson College.* New York: Robert Carter, 1840.

Morrow, Josiah. *The History of Warren County.* Chicago: W.H. Beers Company, 1882.

Nash, Gary B., and Jean R. Soderlund. *Freedom by Degrees: Emancipation in Pennsylvania and Its Aftermath.* New York: Oxford University Press, 1991.

Pennington, James W.C. *The Fugitive Blacksmith, Or, Events in the History of James W.C. Pennington.* London: Charles Gilpin, 1849.

Rupp, I. Daniel. *The History and Topography of Dauphin, Cumberland, Franklin, Bedford, Adams, and Perry Counties.* Lancaster: Gilbert Hills, 1846.

Seward, Frederick W., ed. *William H. Seward: An Autobiography from 1801 to 1834, With a Memoir of His Life, and Selections from His Letters, 1831–1846.* New York: D. Appleton and Company, 1877.

Sharp, Thomas. *Biographical Annals of Cumberland County Pennsylvania.* Chicago: Genealogical Publishing Company, 1905.

Siebert, Wilbur H. *The Underground Railroad from Slavery to Freedom.* New York: MacMillan Company, 1898.

Slotten, Martha C. "The McClintock Slave Riot of 1847." *Cumberland County History* 17, no. 1 (Summer 2000).

Smedley, R.C. *History of the Underground Railroad in Chester and the Neighboring Counties of Pennsylvania.* Lancaster, PA: John A. Hiestand, 1883.

Smith, David G. *On the Edge of Freedom: The Fugitive Slave Issue in South-central Pennsylvania, 1820–1870.* New York: Fordham University Press, 2013.

Still, William. *Still's Underground Railroad Records.* Philadelphia: William Still, 1886.

Sturtevant, P. *The Harrisburg Directory, and Stranger's Guide; with a sketch of the First Settlement of Harrisburg.* Harrisburg, PA: Sturtevant, 1839.

Switala, William J. *Underground Railroad in Pennsylvania.* Mechanicsburg, PA: Stackpole Books, 2001.

Trefousse, Hans L. *Thaddeus Stevens: Nineteenth-Century Egalitarian.* Chapel Hill: University of North Carolina Press, 1997.

Tritt, Richard L., and Randy Watt, eds. *At a Place Called the Boiling Springs.* N.p.: Boiling Springs Sesquicentennial Committee, 1995.

Tully, Alan. "Patterns of Slaveholding in Colonial Pennsylvania: Chester and Lancaster Counties, 1729–1758." *Journal of Social History* 6, no. 3 (Spring 1973).

Turner, Edward Raymond. *The Negro in Pennsylvania: Slavery—Servitude—Freedom, 1639–1861*. Washington, D.C.: The American Historical Association, 1911.

Vaux, Robert. *Memoirs of the Lives of Benjamin Lay and Ralph Sandiford; Two of the Earliest Advocates for the Emancipation of the Enslaved Africans*. Philadelphia: William Phillips, George Yard, 1816.

Vermilyea, Peter C. "The Effect of Lee's Invasion on Gettysburg's African-American Community." *Gettysburg Magazine* no. 24 (January 2001).

Volwiler, Albert T. *George Croghan and the Westward Movement, 1741–1782*. Cleveland, OH: Arthur H. Clark Company, 1926.

Wainwright, Nicholas B. *George Croghan: Wilderness Diplomat*. Chapel Hill: University of North Carolina Press, 1959.

Warner, Beers and Company. *History of Cumberland and Adams Counties, Pennsylvania*. Chicago: Warner, Beers and Company, 1886.

———. *History of Franklin County, Pennsylvania*. Chicago: Warner, Beers and Company, 1887.

Wax, Darold D. "Africans on the Delaware: The Pennsylvania Slave Trade, 1759–1765." *Pennsylvania History* 50, no. 1 (January 1983).

———. "The Demand for Slave Labor in Colonial Pennsylvania." *Pennsylvania History* 34, no. 4 (October 1967).

———. "Negro Imports into Pennsylvania, 1720–1766." *Pennsylvania History* 32, no. 3 (July 1965).

———. "Quaker Merchants and the Slave Trade in Colonial Pennsylvania." *Pennsylvania Magazine of History and Biography* 86, no. 2 (April 1962).

Webber, Christopher L. *American to the Backbone: The Life of James W.C. Pennington*. New York: Pegasus Books, 2011.

Wert, J. Howard. *Episodes of Gettysburg and the Underground Railroad*. Edited by G. Craig Caba. Gettysburg, PA: G. Craig Caba, 1998.

Zilversmit, Arthur. *The First Emancipation: The Abolition of Slavery in the North*. Chicago: University of Chicago Press, 1967.

Government Documents

Bureau of the Census. *Abstract of the Returns of the Fifth Census*. Washington, D.C.: Duff Green, 1832.

———. *Aggregate Amount of Each Description of Persons within the United States of America, and the territories thereof, agreeably to actual enumeration made according to law, in the year 1810*. Washington, D.C.: U.S. Treasury Department, 1811.

———. *Census for 1820*. Washington, D.C.: Gales and Seaton, 1821.

————. *Compendium of the Enumeration of the Inhabitants and Statistics of the United States.* Washington, D.C.: Thomas Allen, 1841.

————. *Heads of Families at the First Census of the United States Taken in the Year 1790.* Washington, D.C.: Government Printing Office, 1908.

————. *Return of the Whole Number of Persons within the Several Districts of the United States.* Washington, D.C.: by order of the House of Representatives, [1801].

Congressional Globe.

Journals of the House of Representatives of the Commonwealth of Pennsylvania. Beginning the twenty-eighth Day of November 1776, and Ending the second Day of October, 1781. Philadelphia: John Dunlap, 1782.

Kennedy, Joseph C.G. *Population of the United States in 1860; Compiled from the Returns of the Eighth Census.* Washington, D.C.: Government Printing Office, 1864.

Minot, George, ed. *The Statutes at Large and Treaties of the United States of America.* Boston: Little, Brown & Company, 1862.

Pennsylvania Archives (1852–1914). 7 Series.

Pennsylvania. *Minutes of the Supreme Executive Council of Pennsylvania, from its Organization to the Termination of the Revolution.* Harrisburg, PA: Theophilus Fenn, 1853.

————. *The Statutes at Large of Pennsylvania from 1682 to 1801.* 14 vols. Harrisburg, PA: William Stanley Ray, 1896–1909.

Manuscripts and Unpublished Documents

African-American Collection, Manuscript Group 72, Cumberland County Historical Society, Carlisle, PA.

Battlefield Farm Properties. Files. Gettysburg National Military Park Library.

Belles Lettres Society Minute Book, Belles Lettres Society, Archives and Special Collections, Dickinson College, Carlisle, PA.

Blair, Nettie Jane. Reminisce. Box 120-13, Cumberland County Historical Society, Carlisle, PA.

Brisben, Esther. Bill of Sale. Haldeman-Wright Family Collection, Manuscript Group 64, Pennsylvania State Archives, Harrisburg, PA.

Callendar, Robert. Last Will and Testament. Book I-164, Allegheny County Register of Wills, Pittsburgh, PA.

Carothers Family, Slave Sale Papers. Box 9-15, Cumberland County Historical Society, Carlisle, PA.

Census Records, Borough of Gettysburg and Cumberland Township. 1860 U.S. Census. Population Schedule. National Archives and Records Administration microfilm M653.

Civilian Claims Files. Gettysburg National Military Park Library.

Codori, Anthony. Deed W-410, Adams County Historical Society, Gettysburg, PA.

"Constitution of the Cumberland County Colonization Society." Broadside. Pamphlet File 2-5, Cumberland County Historical Society, Carlisle, PA.

Estate Inventories. Microfilm at Cumberland County Historical Society, Carlisle, PA.

Gettysburg's African-American Community. File. Gettysburg National Military Park Library.

Hamilton, James, and William Parker. Correspondence. Manuscript Group 34, Cumberland County Historical Society, Carlisle, PA.

Harris, John, Sr. Will File. Historical Society of Dauphin County, Harrisburg, PA.

Harris Trading Post File. Historical Society of Dauphin County, Harrisburg, PA.

Hercules File. Historical Society of Dauphin County, Harrisburg, PA.

Indenture. Jacob to William D. Seymour. Container 008-1, Folder 17b, Cumberland County Historical society, Carlisle, PA.

Indenture. "Negroe Richard" to Isaac Brown Parker. Container 8, Folder 18, Cumberland County Historical society, Carlisle, PA.

Indentured Servant and Apprentice Matters. Papers. Cumberland County Archives, Carlisle, PA.

Insolvent Debtor's Petitions. Papers. Cumberland County Archives, Carlisle, PA.

Jack, Patrick. Bill of Sale. Box 9, Cumberland County Historical Society, Carlisle, PA.

Kirkpatrick, John. Bill of Sale. Box 1-29, Cumberland County Historical Society, Carlisle, PA.

Poorhouse Directors' Statements. Papers. Cumberland County Archives, Carlisle, PA.

"Register of Negroe and Mulatto Slaves & Servants 1780," Lancaster County History, Lancaster, PA.

Register of Negroes and Mulattoes, 1800–1820. Adams County Prothonotary, Gettysburg, PA.

Slave and Slaveholder Register. Cumberland County Archives, Carlisle, PA.

Slave Returns. Papers. Cumberland County Archives, Carlisle, PA.

Slavery File. York County Heritage Trust, York, PA.

Stevens, Thaddeus. File. Adams County Historical Society, Gettysburg, PA.

Tax Records, Cumberland County. Transcripts at Cumberland County Historical Society, Carlisle, PA.

Toombs, Robert, Papers. Hargrett Rare Book and Manuscript Library, University of Georgia.

Underground Railroad File. York County Heritage Trust, York, PA.

Wert, J. Howard, Collection. Private Collection.

Whitehill, Robert. Papers. Cumberland County Historical Society, Carlisle, PA.

Wills. Cumberland County Register of Wills, Carlisle, PA.

Zeamer, Jeremiah Papers. Cumberland County Historical Society, Carlisle, PA.

NEWSPAPERS

Adams Centinel (Gettysburg)

American Volunteer (Carlisle)

American Weekly Mercury (Philadelphia)

Carlisle American

Carlisle Gazette

Carlisle Herald

Chambersburg Valley Spirit

Dauphin Oracle (Harrisburg)

Farmers' Register (Chambersburg)

Franklin Repository (Chambersburg)

Gettysburg Compiler

Harrisburg Telegraph

Niles' Weekly Register (Baltimore)

Pennsylvania Freeman (Philadelphia)

Pennsylvania Gazette (Philadelphia)

Pennsylvania Herald and York General Advertiser

Pennsylvania Packet (Philadelphia)

Pennsylvania Republican and Democratic Herald (Harrisburg)

Star and Republican Banner (Gettysburg)

York Recorder

INDEX

ABOUT THE AUTHOR

Cooper Wingert is the author of ten books and numerous articles on slavery and the American Civil War. He is the recipient of the 2012 Dr. James I. Robertson, Jr. Literary Award for Confederate History in recognition for his book *The Confederate Approach on Harrisburg*.

Visit us at
www.historypress.net
....
This title is also available as an e-book